P9-BJG-400

# Advance Praise for Life Speaks

"In *Life Speaks*, Cathy takes us on a journey that outlines only a portion of the deep learning she has gained. Using her own growth experiences – often achieved by significant adventures in her own life – Cathy helps us see the beginning of the process of transformation for which so many of us long.

I encourage you to savor these words. Trust and explore what they stir in you. You won't be sorry."

— *Sharon Henwood, Artist*

"If your old way of looking at your life is no longer working for you and you've tried everything, Cathy's easy, charming, grounded style will help you see that the solution is so much simpler than you could imagine. Simple, not easy. A deeply profound and moving book."

— *Christine Buhr, Entrepreneur, Mom*

"Cathy has successfully helped me to generate a deep and abiding trust in my own intuition. I am so glad to see that Cathy's soulful, heart-centered methods have been captured in book form so her genius can now be shared with the world at large. If you have done everything you were supposed to in your life and you're still not happy, this book is for you."

— *Karen Rowe, #1 International Bestselling Author*

"This book is like a warm breeze on a cool night under a sky filled with starry possibilities! With conviction, compassion and humor Cathy will help you to see the opportunities through the obstacles. *Life Speaks* will resonate deep in your soul and you will feel as though you were walking beside her through every word."

— *Debra L. Rogers*

"Be prepared to get back on track. If you are seeking to live, work and flourish at a higher level, this book can take you there."

— *Leanne Cherry, Talent Director*

"Cathy shares hard won insights, using real life examples and gives us a guide to living the life we were meant to live. A must read!"

— *Cheryl Stiefvater*

"Join the author on her literal and metaphoric walk through the mountains…In a compassionate, yet fierce voice, Cathy cuts to the chase on the importance of letting go of expectations, and trusting your intuition. Relevant, real and easy to relate to, 'Life Speaks' will activate your own inner knowing and inspire you to listen."

— *PattiWardlaw, Owner, Practicing Grace Qigong*

"Cathy Yost writes every word directly from her genuine, loving and wise heart. The truth of her soul reveals itself as a generous gift for those who have the opportunity to flip these pages. *Life Speaks* is a must-read for those looking for guidance with a heart-felt touch."

— *Nadine Nicholson, PCC, The Time Management Expert, MeJane.ca*

"Cathy gently reminds us, with natural wisdom, that our greatest challenges & setbacks are indeed our greatest allies and that life is always on our side."

— *Janelle Morrison, Professional-triathlete-turned-Mind-Body-Coach*

"In *Life Speaks*, Cathy uses her own courageous story to teach us the importance of trusting our intuition, living our values, and taking off the mask of who we think we should be in order to truly show up in our own lives. This book will make you laugh, it will make you cry and it will make you reflect on a deep level about your own life."

— *Danielle Reed, Coach on the Go*

*To Bruce*

# life
# speaks

*Challenging Moments Are*
*Our Greatest Gifts*

*With gratitude!*

*Cathy* :)

CATHY YOST

Copyright © 2016 Red Tulip Publishing

All rights reserved. The scanning, uploading, and electronic sharing of any part of this book without the permission of the publisher is unlawful piracy and theft of the author's intellectual property. Please purchase only authorized editions, and do not participate in or encourage electronic piracy of copyrighted materials. If you would like to use material from this book (other than for review purposes), prior written permission must be obtained by contacting the author at Cathy@LifeSpeaks.ca

Thank you for your support of this author's rights.

Limit of Liability / Disclaimer of Warranty: While the publisher and author have used their best efforts in preparing the book, they make no representations or warranties with respect to the accuracy or completeness of the contents of this book and specifically disclaim any implied warranties of merchantability or fitness for a particular purpose. No warranty may be created or extended by sales representatives or written sales materials. The advice and strategies contained herein may not be suitable for your situation. You should consult with a professional where appropriate.

Managing Editor and Project Management: Karen Rowe, Front Rowe Seat Communications, karen@karenrowe.com
Editor: Julia Petrisor, BeLoved Words, juliapetrisor.com
Cover Design: Shake Creative, shaketampa.com

Printed in Canada
FIRST EDITION

ISBN: 978-0-9953179

Published by Red Tulip Publishing

*This book is dedicated to my children,*
*Chris and Becky*
*who inspire me beyond belief,*
*and are still my greatest teachers.*

We must let go of the life we have planned,
so as to accept the one that is waiting for us.

– *Joseph Campbell*

# Table of Contents

# Acknowledgements & Gratitude

This book has been waiting in the wings for a decade or more for me to write, and yet it is a collaboration of love inspired by many very talented individuals. Words cannot express how I feel about each one of you who have stood beside me through this journey.

Melanie Jones, you wouldn't let up until I wrote this book, even dragging me to NYC to do it! I couldn't have written a word without you cheering me on. Your courage and tenacity in everything you do never ceases to amaze and inspire me.

My beLoved editor Julia Petrisor, you seemed to understand the words and the story I was trying to tell even before I did. You are one talented lady and I loved working with you! We make a good team.

Karen Rowe, it's come full circle – three days of magic! My managing editor; thank you for guiding me through this amazing process from conception to birth. You are my literary mid-wife. Your wisdom and brilliance kept this baby moving forward and out into the world. I am in awe of how easy you make it.

Sharon Henwood, I am honored to showcase your beautiful artwork on the back cover. Three decades of your love and friendship has meant the world to me.

My reading posse Shelly Grubbe, Debra Rogers and Donna Phillips. I am forever grateful for your comments, suggestions and encouragement in its fledgeling form... This story is richer because of you.

To my Mom, who pushed me into the world long before I was ready, to teach me fearlessness: Whether I took flight or came crashing to the ground, you stood by me believing my strength and character would get me through and teach me what I needed to learn. As painful as it was, it worked! Your unconditional love and unwavering devotion will forever touch my soul.

I want to thank my teachers and mentors, Louise Hay, Julia Cameron, Brené Brown, Eckhart Tolle, Pamela Wilson and Richard Dolan – your unique blend of teachings always inspire me to do better and go farther.

And thank you to the countless clients who have inspired me over the years to share this work and my perspective beyond our sessions.

Lastly, I want to acknowledge my relationships I speak of throughout the book. Without you I wouldn't have learned what I needed to, or grown from these experiences. My most challenging moments have been my greatest gifts, and I am forever grateful to you for them.

# A Note to Readers

# 'You didn't come this far to only come this far.'

Ask someone who has survived a life-threatening illness – someone who has been given a second chance at life – whether or not their most challenging moment was the biggest gift to their life's mission. They will tell you it was. Some may even say it was the best thing that ever happened to them. Ask someone who has experienced a lay-off or a set-back in their career – to suddenly have a new opportunity awaiting them on the other side – whether they are glad it happened. They will tell you they are. Ask someone whose relationship has gone sour – to afterwards meet the true love of their life – whether they can imagine life without that person. They will tell you they can't.

Have you ever wondered why you attract the same type of lover over and over again, why your new boss has similar qualities to your last, why your friends treat you the same way as your annoying siblings? The adversity we face, people that rub us the wrong way, a situation or relationship that we don't like, a place we don't want to be: it may seem easier to run away than to face them head on. But these moments are here for you.

When we turn and run away from the person, the situation, the challenge, the adversity, we miss the opportunity to learn and grow. We miss the gift it is bringing.

I've heard it say we are all spiritual beings having human experience. What does that mean? In my best definition, it means we are all here to learn the lessons we are here to learn whilst we are here. Yes, we're here to live our lives, go to work, raise our children, marry – all of those delicious things – but we're also here to grow our spirit and learn from our mistakes. Whether it's a divorce, an illness, a tragedy – these are all opportunities to pull the gift out and use them for our good.

A course I took early on in my career taught us that if we look at our wounds as teachers, they will become our greatest wisdom. It's hard to grasp. How can something that has hurt me be the very thing that heals me?

This book is my answer to that question. It has happened to you for reasons you may not know yet. But they are your greatest gifts, if you choose to stand in the fire and face them. Trust the process. These experiences are uniquely yours, and only you have your perspective and distinct wisdom. Other people are looking for that, and needing it as well.

The world needs you. The world needs your gifts. We're hurting and we need to stand together.

Stand in the fire, with your brothers and sisters who also do their inner work, and be the light. This book is my gift to you. Take my hand, let's go on this journey together.

# life speaks

## Chapter 1

# A Whisper, a Feather,
# or a Two-by-Four?

Cathy awoke that morning to the sun streaming into her bedroom. It was barely 6:30 am and already a warm late summer morning. She lay in bed a moment, listening to the birds chirping. She paused and took a deep breath. She felt an extraordinary sensation wash over her – one that was not fully familiar. She took another breath and exhaled fully. The sensation remained. Yes, she knew what it was.

She felt at peace.

Cathy sat up in bed and picked up her journal from the bedside table. She began to write. She wrote quickly and with a keen sense of fulfillment. She was so grateful. This peaceful feeling was beginning to be familiar. It hadn't always been that way.

Over the course of the morning, Cathy remained attuned to her feelings and noticed the ebb and flow of peace. It was as if she were waiting for it to pass; as if she knew it just couldn't last. As it lasted into most of that morning, she slowly began to let her guard down.

"Okay, peace," Cathy said to herself. "I welcome you and hope you find a nice place to stay. And I get it – you'll come and go. Thanks for showing up today."

Cathy smiled to herself. Her little scruffy terrior mix, Ellie, fresh from her early morning snooze, wandered over to her and rubbed her legs. Cathy looked down at her.

"What do you think, Ellie?" Cathy said, reaching down to scratch her behind her ears. "I think it's time for a walk, don't you?"

At the word "walk," Ellie's ears perked up and she reached her paws up and onto Cathy's shins.

Cathy gathered Ellie's collar and leash and was just about out the door when the phone rang.

"Hello?" Cathy answered.

"Cathy?" It was Cathy's friend, Pamela. "Are you free?"

Cathy could tell from the tone of Pamela's voice that she was having one of her days. Cathy recognized it all too well – she had been there, after all. Pamela was overworked, in a stressful relationship with two young children, and trying to balance work and household life. She was trying to be the perfect mom, perfect partner, and perfect CFO of the large company she worked for. Cathy could only empathize. She remembered all too well what those days were like. She settled into her chair to listen.

"Sure," Cathy said. "Are you okay?"

Cathy heard Pamela take a breath. "I don't know, Cathy." She heard Pamela sniffle. She sounded like she was trying to hold back tears. Cathy waited for Pamela to talk.

Pamela finally spoke. "Well... I don't know where to begin."

Cathy waited, silent on her end of the line.

Cathy heard Pamela sniffle a bit and then take another deep breath. "Okay," she started slowly. "Last week, I found a lump in my breast."

Cathy nodded and frowned. "Oh dear," she said simply.

Pamela went on. "Tomorrow I go in for the biopsy."

"Okay..." Cathy said, not wanting to interrupt.

"This morning, when I woke up, I just... I just felt so scared. Cathy, I'm terrified. What if I have breast cancer? What will my kids do? I can't... Cathy, I can't..." Pamela started to cry again.

Cathy felt an outpouring of empathy for her friend. She felt a pull to help, yet also to allow Pamela the opportunity to grow. As she listened, Cathy looked out the window. It was a beautiful day. The temperature was just right, and it was sunny and hot with a light breeze. She had an idea.

"Pamela, where are you right now?"

Pamela blew her nose. "I'm at work. I had to come in for a meeting."

"You're still at the office?" Cathy asked.

"Yes."

"What do you think about taking the rest of the day off?"

"I couldn't..." Pamela said. Her voice moved from soft to business-like in an instant. "No, I can't. I need to be here."

Cathy prodded gently. "What would it feel like to take the rest of the day off?"

"No, no..." Pamela started.

Cathy cut her off. "Just think about it, right now, while I'm on the phone."

Pamela was quiet. After a few moments, she answered. "It feels like…relief."

"What do you need to do to take the day off? Who do you need to tell?"

"Well, just Jim, really. He can tell the staff."

"Then I have an idea. Take the afternoon off. I'll be at your place in a half hour. Got it?"

Pamela tried to laugh. "Okay." She repeated herself, a little stronger this time. "Okay. I'm doing it."

"Good. I'll pick you up in a half hour – be ready for a hike."

Pamela managed a laugh this time. "I don't know about that, Cathy!" she said. Before hanging up, Pamela added one last thing. "Cathy?"

"Yes?" Cathy said.

"Thank you."

Cathy laughed. "You can thank me later. See you in a bit!"

# Chapter 2

# Falling Apart

When Cathy arrived, Pamela was still in tears. She answered the door, still dressed in her business clothes. She was wearing a power suit of navy blue cotton with a light white linen blouse. She was quite the sight – this tall, striking woman in a suit made for the conference room, with a red, puffy face streaming with tears. Cathy walked in and gave her friend a hug.

As they released their embrace, Cathy looked Pamela up and down. "I'm thinking you should change your clothes. We're going to the mountains."

Pamela nodded and laughed weakly. She went upstairs to change.

Moments later, Pamela came down, clad in the spotlessly clean, contemporary sporty yoga clothes most working mothers wore in their downtime. Her hair was pulled up into a perfect ponytail with not a hair out of place. She had splashed her face with water and washed off her makeup. Even in her leisure wear, Pamela looked powerful and stunning.

"That's better," Cathy said. "Let's go walk it out."

They headed out, Ellie following close at Cathy's side.

They arrived at the trailhead and began to walk side by side on the trail. Pamela started walking at a very fast pace, leaving Cathy behind.

"Wow, Pamela!" Cathy commented. "Are you in a rush?" She winked at Pamela.

Pamela stopped and laughed. "Oh, I hadn't even noticed! Was I walking really fast? You know, the kids tell me all the time when we're hiking, 'Slow down, Mom!' I guess I'm always moving fast."

"Well, here's your chance to slow things down, because I know I don't walk that fast." Cathy paused and looked around, sweeping her arms up at the view. "And I don't want to! Look where we are!"

Cathy took a deep breath of fresh air and noticed that she still felt peace.

Pamela, noticing Cathy, tried to take a deep breath too, but she stopped short. "I can't do it," she said.

"Can't do what?" Cathy asked.

"I can't take a deep breath." Pamela looked at Cathy, scared.

"Okay. First of all, you can, just not in this exact moment. And maybe in this moment, you don't need to. Why don't you just talk? Just talk."

Pamela nodded and calmed herself down. She began to talk.

"You know, I just don't get it, Cathy. Throughout our lives we're taught to keep everything under control. As women especially, we're taught to be nice, to not cause any waves, and certainly, for men and women alike, to not show our emotions. Certainly, don't ever show anybody that you're vulnerable or that you might have something that's not working in your life that is just falling apart." She looked at Cathy and whispered, feeling tears threatening to interrupt her, "Cathy, I think I'm falling apart."

Cathy nodded.

Pamela went on, "I can't do it anymore, Cathy. I just want to run away. I want to numb myself. The pain… I can't make everyone happy. I can't even make myself happy. I try so hard, every day. I work so hard. I make healthy dinners for the family. I put everyone else first. Their needs. What's best for them. It's just too much. Is this who I am? I don't even recognize myself."

Cathy gently explained, "This pain – it's trying to get your attention. It's not who you are. You've lived your life according to the rules, right? And now you can't do it anymore. You can't go back."

"Except I don't even know where I am. I don't even know what I'm supposed to do. Why is there a lump in my breast? Things like this don't happen to me. I eat salad every day, for goodness' sake!" Pamela shook her head, tears coming to her eyes. "I'm just so scared, Cathy."

Cathy replied, "That's understandable – of course you're scared. And maybe you can't hear this in this moment, but your life is trying to wake you up, and all of the messages at this point are trying to get your attention. This is the first step of your makeover."

"Makeover? What do I need to makeover? Who or what will I turn into?"

Cathy just smiled and looked ahead to a grove of pines they were about to enter. "I don't know! You may not even know. I do know this, however: All of this is an invitation to change—in other words, a transformation—if you're open to it."

"Transformation? That scares me!"

Cathy shrugged. "Fear of change is what holds us back from making any adjustments at all in our life. We would rather stay in an uncomfortable situation than make waves or make any changes. Change can be very scary. We don't know what's on the other side. Familiar is comfortable. It may not be ideal, but it's known. There's some sort of relief about the idea that if we just keep things the same, maybe things will change on their own, and that we don't have to take the action." Cathy paused for a moment, letting her words sink in. Then she asked Pamela, "Are you afraid to look at your life and see what's not working?"

Pamela nodded. "Yes. I can't even imagine doing anything else with my life. If I change, what will happen? I can't stop working. I have worked so hard to get to this place. I love my kids. My husband and I love each other, even if it isn't great at times. I don't want to move. Change isn't an option!"

"I hate to be the one to break it to you, but your life is begging you to change. So yes, you may need to change…something, at least. As a personal coach, I saw so many clients who were so afraid of change that they took no action. They were totally afraid to make any waves in their lives. For some of them it was easier to take anti-depressants, or use alcohol or drugs to numb the pain this inaction was causing.

"I have a question for you, Pamela. Have you ever wondered what your life might be like if you could relax and simply be happy?"

Pamela kept looking down at the trail as she walked. "I… I don't know."

Cathy took a deep breath of pine and let it fill her up. "When was the last time you felt calm and happy for no reason?"

Pamela stopped on the trail to think. Ellie had run ahead, and was waiting a few yards along, wondering why they weren't walking.

After a few moments, Pamela's eyes welled up with tears. "Honestly?" she asked.

"Honestly," Cathy said.

"I think I was 12." Pamela started to cry. "It was the summer when I was 12, and I felt so free. I had no responsibilities. Before I became a teenager and got a parttime job. I remember everything changing once I entered junior high." Pamela closed her eyes. "How can that be the last time I felt happy?"

Cathy said gently. "You are not alone my friend. So many of us don't honor what makes us happy in our lives. We just give ourselves away. We go along with many uncomfortable situations and what society expects of us. We don't speak up at work, or in our marriages or friendships. We aren't honest with ourselves."

Pamela just listened, crying quietly, as she walked beside Cathy.

Cathy continued, "At the end of the day, you have to face you. You have to sleep with you. You have to live with you every single day. You have to look in the mirror, and ask yourself, 'What's the cost of silencing myself and selling out?' What's the cost of not honoring what you know is right for you? Eventually it may erode your soul, and it costs you your sleep. Believe me, I know. Inevitably it will cost you your joy, your fulfillment and your passion. Your purpose for being here becomes muddled, and you begin to question what's the point? This is what we sacrifice for staying silent, for not honoring our truth, for not honoring who we are and for not honoring what we know to be true. We accept the role – it's what we do and becomes our way of life and it's all we know. By that point, to make change or even make a decision seems like the most foreign and scary thing that we'll ever do."

Cathy was silent for a moment.

Pamela asked, "Have you ever felt this way?"

Cathy nodded. "A long time ago, before I knew you."

Pamela asked, "What happened?"

Cathy sighed lightly. "Well, it's a long story."

"I'm listening," Pamela said.

# Chapter 3

# Who is in the Mirror?

They hiked together, Cathy every so often prompting Pamela to slow down. It was clear that Pamela could not relax. She treated the hike like a race; each hill was a new conquest. When Cathy could be successful at slowing her down, they'd walk side by side until Pamela's pace crept up. Cathy just let it be, watching the ebb and flow of Pamela's pace as it matched the ebb and flow of their conversation.

They crested the top of the next hill and Cathy paused to look around at the view. She loved this trail, this hike. Just being here reminded her how far she had come in her own life. She was about to share her story with her friend, and suddenly realized she was finally in a place where she could recognize the gifts of her experiences and feel total gratitude for them.

"As I approached 40," Cathy began, "I started to feel I no longer recognized who I was or the life I created for myself. It was like I had awoken from a long, deep sleep, and when I did, everything was a dream. My perspective of my life had changed. I no longer saw things the way I used to. I saw a new perspective. And the skin I was in no longer fit. I speak of this time as a cruel joke and a gift at the same time. I saw myself living someone else's life; it was someone else's dream and someone else's image of who I was.

"One day I woke up, and my life did not look recognizable. It made absolutely no sense to me at all; the work I was doing, how my husband and I were raising our two kids—a boy and a girl— together. It all looked perfect from the outside, but on the inside I felt empty and alone. I felt like something had shifted within me, and I was the only one that got the memo. My husband hadn't changed, but I had."

"How, though? If you were still working, and married, how did you change?" Pamela asked.

It was clear that to Pamela, change was big-picture; external. She couldn't understand the subtle ways change manifests. "I felt like everything I was living up to that point was a lie. I didn't know what the truth was. I made him bad and wrong for everything he did. I made everything about my career bad and wrong. I didn't know what to do. The only thing I knew to do was to run. I decided that my kids and I would leave. We would leave all of that carnage behind and start all over. I would find a new life because all of those things – they were what was wrong. It was not my fault."

Pamela listened attentively. Cathy could tell that although she didn't necessarily understand the depth of Cathy's change, Pamela nonetheless understood exactly how Cathy had felt.

"Ironically, at the same time, my husband gifted me a copy of Julia Cameron's The Artist's Way. Unbeknownst to him, that simple gift changed my life, and ultimately led me to end my relationship with him. It flung me onto a spiritual journey that I didn't even know I wanted to take."

"Really? I have never heard of her. What did you learn?" Pamela asked.

Cathy continued, "Oh, a dam of feelings simply burst and my whole world opened up! It was as if I had woken up from a 40-year sleep and it flung me into a life of new discoveries which in turn caused turmoil, uncertainty and change. She wrote about inspiring and unleashing your creativity by silencing your inner critic. You know, that negative voice we all have – for me, that voice was telling me that I was not good enough, smart enough, pretty enough... whatever enough. Her 12-week course helped me explore the idea that I could create my own creative and joy-filled life. Something stirred deep within me as I read that book. It lead me to completely blow up my life as I knew it."

"Blow up your life?"

"Yes! Once I took off my rose-colored glasses and saw things for the way they were, versus how I wanted them to be, I could no longer un-see. Everything from that point on changed profoundly. I began to question the status quo. I began to explore what made me happy and what things I liked to do. I researched new and different ways of raising our kids, because the way we were raising them didn't feel comfortable for me. I found the work of Barbara Coloroso. She spoke my language. It was as if she knew what I was going through and had solutions to make peace and bring harmony into my family.

"I wish I could say everyone in the household embraced the change, however that wasn't the case. Raising kids with firm boundaries and natural consequences made total sense to me. I remember feeling like I was an anomaly, upholding this concept in a world of overprotective parents. Allowing them the freedom to choose and to make mistakes while holding them responsible for their choices, I trusted, would teach them to make different and better decisions for themselves then and in the future. It was brilliant. Our motto was, 'Say it, mean it, do it.' Meaning, you are held accountable to your word.

"I was also working 14 hour days in the film industry which eventually took its toll on my marriage and my sanity. I remember often times I felt like my dog was the only person who understood me!" Both women laughed and Ellie perked up her ears as Cathy said the word "dog."

"Yes, Bayleigh—my dog at the time—she loved me unconditionally and without judgment. After a long day, I'd take her out for a run. Just like I do with you, El!" Cathy said to Ellie, who had run back to Cathy on the trail, looking for a scratch behind the ears. Cathy bent down and gave Ellie a scratch, and Ellie ran off again.

Cathy continued, "Truthfully, I ran myself into a divorce. Running was cathartic. It was my time to sort out my thoughts and make sense of how I was feeling. I eventually gathered strength to make new choices. In the end my husband and I agreed to disagree and parted ways, amicably. We agreed to raise our kids together, yet apart. There were times when I would think, Why am I doing this? Things aren't that bad. We can stay together until our youngest leaves home.

"But you know when something is all muddled and doesn't make any sense at the time, and then suddenly it's like a light switch flips and voila – it all makes perfect sense afterward?" Pamela nodded. "That's what happened when we decided to end our marriage. It felt like there was a hand pushing me out the door. …literally."

They crossed a bridge over a small, fast river, and stopped to watch the river flowing beneath them. Cathy went on, "But you know what was really interesting? Once I had committed to that decision, everything just started to naturally fall into place. A family heard we may sell our house, knocked on our door and bought it on the spot. I found the perfect house for my kids and I in the price range I could afford and the separation seemed seamless. For me, at least. My kids were amazing, and their Dad was the best ex-husband on the planet. We had a few growing pains—even a few struggles— but all in all it was the best way to raise two individuals who are now brilliant, independent, self-sufficient and responsible, happy adults."

Pamela and Cathy watched the river. "I guess it was a happy story, in the end?" Pamela asked. "I just don't know. I don't think I want to get a divorce, but I don't know what else to do. I don't know what to change."

Cathy said, "I am not saying that you need to get a divorce. Your body is simply telling you that you need to make a change. Maybe your health is all that needs attention. Maybe the job." She turned to Pamela suddenly, and asked, "Do you believe you are responsible for your life?"

Pamela shrugged, "I don't know. I think things keep happening to me and I have to deal with them."

"Maybe, but what if you actually have the potential to create what happens to you?" Cathy asked.

Pamela shook her head. "Ahhhh… I don't think so. I'm pretty sure we don't have that kind of control. After all, if we did, why would so many bad things happen in the world?"

Cathy smiled. "Let me tell you, I once would have agreed with you. In fact, I remember getting a copy of Louise Hay's *You Can Heal Your Life* shortly after reading *The Artist's Way*."

"Louise Hay? Who's she?"

"Oh, she is an incredible pioneer in the self-help community. She explains how our physical illness and disease are linked to our negative emotions and beliefs. It's a bit hard to swallow at first; however, you see how powerful the mind and body connection is in the body healing itself. When you realize how much power you have to affect your own health, it changes everything.

"It's a mind-blowing concept. When I first got the book, I'm pretty sure I threw it across the room. I didn't want to believe it. I even used it as a window prop, so it got soaked in the rain and became unreadable." Cathy chuckled. "How can you be that responsible for your life and your well being? Years later it came back to me, and this time I was ready to hear her message.

"When I started to do my personal work, I realized that the buck stopped here with me. I took a powerful personal development weekend workshop. One of the sessions in the workshop involved making all of my wrongs right by acknowledging and taking full responsibility for my actions or inactions. This meant cleaning up everything in my life – all of my tarnished relationships. I started by calling my ex-husband and apologizing for my part in the demise of our relationship. It was really difficult. I apologized to my kids for the mistakes I made and told them how much I loved them. I called everyone from my Mom to friends – everyone who I had left in my wake. I had the epiphany that I was the one who was at the source of everything I had created, good or bad. This unleashed an enormous amount of power and freedom; and it also caused a lot of heartbreak. I realized I had shattered others' lives by making them bad and wrong. I was simply trying protect myself and run from what didn't feel good. Really, I was just trying to make myself feel better. And I did, for a while. Yet it followed me and would always come up to bite me.

"It's impossible to run away from yourself because wherever you go, there you are." Cathy laughed.

Cathy went on, "The hardest part for me to see was that I couldn't blame anybody. Not that I wanted to instead blame myself—although I did that for a while too—but I started to see my life from a different perspective and see that everything in my life was happening for me, not to me."

Pamela shook her head again. "I'm not sure. How can you believe that? I'm pretty sure this lump in my breast is happening to me. All the work stress – it's also happening to me. I'm certain of it. In what world would it be good for me to have to deal with staff who lose clients constantly? Or even my family – with one kid on the autism spectrum? I certainly would not have chosen those things. Why would I choose those things?"

Cathy looked at Pamela with a questioning expression. "All I know is that, for me, once I realized I was at the root of everything in my life because of my choices or my lack of choices, which are still choices, it gave me an incredible sense of knowing that I have everything within me to be safe, to be self-sufficient and to be happy. That I don't have to look for something on the outside to either make me happy or make me unhappy. My view—my perception—merely reflected back to me more of what I believe about myself and the world. Through my filter, or lens, in which I saw, the world would inevitably reflect back to me those very experiences I was expecting. It would prove me right every time. My life would mirror my beliefs.

"After this I got really honest about who I was versus who I thought I was, who I wanted to be or who I was expected to be. I didn't want to be seen as weak, or as someone who didn't have it all figured out. I tried very hard to make it all look easy and effortless, all the while running myself ragged and never taking time for myself.

"I was actually running away from who I didn't want to be."

Pamela was silent.

"Really, I'm not sure we are that much different, you and I," Cathy said. "I was trying to be perfect – the perfect wife, perfect Mom, perfect employee, perfect friend, daughter…it goes on and on."

Pamela nodded and laughed, "Boy, can I relate to that!"

"I was running as fast as I could, trying to be everything to everyone. Yet, I was nothing to myself. I was really stretched and torn and maxed out. Trying to be something I wasn't was such hard work. Once I stopped trying to be everything to everybody, I didn't know who I was or how to be anything to me."

Pamela nodded as she listened. "I think that part makes sense. I don't know how to be anything to me, right now, that's for sure. But I know how to be a good mother, a great CFO, and a pretty good partner. I can put out a full course Christmas dinner without breaking a sweat."

Cathy pushed a little, "Although I would argue that the lump in your breast is, really, you starting to break a sweat."

Pamela thought for a minute. "Ohhh. Yes, I never thought of it that way."

Cathy shared, "This may be an invitation for you to take a closer look at your life and at what's not working. An invitation to possibly make a change, an adjustment. For me, as the perception of my life changed, I shifted my priorities and began to put my own needs first. I started taking better care of myself spiritually and physically. I tapped into my own sense of self-worth. This was completely foreign to me. I had been taking care of my family, everyone else and my career for so long, I didn't know that I could transfer that energy to myself. Yet, that's what I needed to do. I needed to take care of me because without doing so, life was empty and meaningless. Nothing else mattered. You've heard the saying, 'If mama ain't happy, nobody's happy?' It's so true."

Cathy paused a moment, and then asked Pamela, "How can you give to your family if you're not healthy or if you're bedridden or hospitalized for months?"

Pamela listened and was quiet. "I…I never thought of it that way," she said, finally. "But I can't imagine… I make more money than Daryl. I can't possibly stop working."

Cathy nodded. "I know how you feel. It's a scary proposition. I totally get it. While my marriage was collapsing, which is enough to bring anyone to their knees, my career was also slowly slipping between my fingers. I had been working in film and television for a couple of decades. I was reaching the next level in my career, and excited by the possibilities of new challenges. However, the degree of my angst and unhappiness, plus being torn between family and career, was speaking to me in a very loud voice. And the money… there was a lot of money coming my way, which made it very difficult to walk away from. Yet with each project I was still taking on more responsibility and more pressure. As I continued to wake up to my life, I recognized that the projects I was working on were not aligning with who I felt I really was. They all left me feeling frantic and disconnected. I kept trying to fit a square peg into a round hole. It wasn't working. I was just feeling more and more disconnected and felt more pain, but was trying harder and harder to make that peg fit in that hole, and I couldn't."

Pamela walked silently. She knew exactly what Cathy was talking about, only she didn't let on.

Cathy continued, "Finally, the torment got so great and it just got so overwhelming that I chose to leave the industry. I left without knowing what I was going to do next. I had let go of one branch before grabbing onto another. It's generally understood, particularly about leaving a job, that you need to line up other work before quitting. In other words, line up that branch. But you can't have both branches in your hands, otherwise you'd just be dangling in the middle of nowhere. Without actually knowing what I was doing, I let go of one branch. I let go of my career."

Pamela asked in disbelief, "You just quit? Just like that? What did you do? How did you make money?"

Cathy smiled, "Well, I really felt that I needed to be in a place that nurtured my spirit during this tender process. I was extremely vulnerable during this time, with so much uncertainty. I really didn't know what was going to happen next. I wanted to be there for my kids and I still needed to work while going through this transition, so I took a part-time job as a Barista at a local coffee shop. It was like coming home to a warm hug each day!"

With that, Cathy paused for effect. Pamela's reaction was not surprising.

Pamela gasped, "Oh my god, Cathy, you didn't! I could never! What a – what a step backwards!"

Cathy just smiled again, "You'd be surprised, my friend!" Pamela just shook her head.

# Chapter 4

# Coffee Brings Clarity!

"It was my solace. This cozy coffee shop in a beautiful log cabin where people would come in at the same time every day almost to the minute to order their favorite latte or french-press coffee. I really believe they mostly came in to connect with people. There were many days the regulars would spend time around the counter and we would engage in a lively discussion. They would tell me about their day or a challenge they were having or just about something that was going on in their life. Oftentimes I would just listen. Then, as I got more comfortable with the group I would offer a different way to look at the challenges they were facing. Sometimes this different perspective would land favorably, and sometimes not, depending on their level of openness. They didn't necessarily want anybody to fix it or to give them any kind of solution. I found many just wanted to know that they were heard, understood and valued. It was quite a learning experience for me."

"Hah, you must have loved the coffee, too," Pamela chuckled.

Cathy just laughed and went on. "Oh, I became quite a coffee connoisseur, although I seemed to spend a lot more of my time connecting with the customers than pouring coffee." She giggled. "It seemed really important to me, though, and it felt right. One day I said to my colleague as we were cleaning up the machines for the day, 'You know, if I could help people and not have to pour coffee, I would be the happiest person in the world.'"

"Like a therapist," Pamela said.

"Well, not quite, but similar, I suppose. Anyway, a short time later, a woman came across the counter and said, 'Cathy, there's a course I think you should take.' Without knowing any other details, in the moment I said, 'Yes.' The woman looked at me and said, 'You didn't even ask what the course was!' I knew I hadn't, but it felt right. I felt like I needed to say yes. I didn't know what I was saying yes to. It turned out to be the beginning of my coaching process."

"Ah, so that's how you became a coach." Pamela mused.

"Well, the story gets better," Cathy said. "That program was a blend of Virginia Satir Family Therapist material combined with Louise Hay teachings. Of course, once I heard the name 'Louise Hay,' I thought, crap, not her again!"

"Right, the one who says we're responsible for our lives."

"Exactly. In this course we learned that the pain we had endured in our life was there to teach us. We were taught that everything that happened in our life—all the pain, the challenges and the heartache—whatever it was, it was all there to teach us, like a gift. And it was up to us whether we would learn and grow from this experience or become or remain the victim. Life speaks to us. All of our choices, or lack of choices, are right here in this moment. There's incredible power in knowing that, yet it's hard to wrap your head around too. Are we not the victims to what has happened to us? My training was with a dozen or more Native American health professionals, who had endured a lot of abuse and mistreatment – how can that be for their good? And what about my challenges? They weren't nearly as painful as what they had endured. We were shown that if you don't learn and grow from your experiences and the pain, then you will forever fall victim and look for someone else to blame. By having that belief you will attract more of those types of people into your life, which ultimately gives them power over you. Yet when you take what you've been given and find a way to forgive, you can then use it for your good, and you are able to live free and in joy. The gifts of the past are there to teach us what we need to let go of, so we are able to move on.

"We were under the microscope every day when we were in class. Our behaviors, patterns and beliefs were all being challenged. Since we were together day and night we couldn't hide or run away from it in the evening either. We were called out on our behavior the next day in the group, which meant we had to face our stuff in front of everyone. We had to take off the masks that we had worn when we were pretending to be who we weren't. It was like lying on the floor naked, being completely exposed and not being able to find your clothes to hide. It was excruciatingly uncomfortable."

"Sounds terrifying, actually," Pamela said, shuddering.

"Despite the difficulty, this course was the wish I had put out to the universe; it came back in that form. This course eventually led me to my formal coach training, which led me to living in Australia and working with my first client."

"Australia? Cathy, I've known you for years and I had no idea about any of this." Pamela just laughed. "Goes to show you what a good listener you are. And how much I blather, apparently."

Cathy just smiled at Pamela and nodded slightly. "I've always enjoyed hearing others talk more than listening to my own voice, and I don't always share everything all the time." She paused a moment to regather her thoughts. "Where was I?"

"Australia – and your first client."

"Right. So, what's fascinating is that I could never have figured it out if it hadn't been for all of the random pebbles along the path – the pebbles being the actions I took leading to this point: Letting go of my film career, the divorce, the coffee shop, the random wish! Besides, I had never heard of coaching, let alone Virginia Satir or the course I took. When I said yes to this program without even knowing what it was, my whole world opened up. I entered into an entirely new and different perspective. Back then this was pretty uncharted territory, and it was scary. As I tried to explain to my friends and family that I wanted to explore this next piece in my life as a career, it sounded just as crazy to me as it did to them. I couldn't make sense of it. Yet, I knew with every fiber of my being that this was the path that I needed to go down."

Pamela listened, fully attentive, as Cathy went on. "After the course, I decided to dip back into the film industry one more time, just to see if it was an option to return to it, or to see if I should leave it permanently. I took a short film project out of town. After completing the project, it was very clear to me I needed to find a new passion. With that decision behind me, I went on a bit of an adventure with my boyfriend, and took the ferry to Salt Spring Island. While strolling through the lovely streets of one of the towns, I saw a poster stapled to a telephone pole. Something caught my eye. It was announcing a personal workshop led by a life coach. A what? I'd never heard of a life coach. Whatever that was, I knew I wanted to be one. Again, just like the earlier course, this course really spoke to me. When I returned home I looked up 'life coaching' and what came up blew me away. It was a profession I had never heard of, yet it felt like it was meant for me. There were even schools devoted to training life coaches. One in particular really spoke to me."

"I've heard of life coaches, but I have always thought they were too...I don't know, 'out there' for me."

Cathy laughed, "Years ago, when I started, many people thought that too, but over the years it has become a very meaningful and respected profession. You're talking to one right now. Do you think I'm 'out there?'"

Pamela shook her head, "No, you're helping me see things differently. I like that." She paused on the trail and tried to take a deep breath again. This time it worked. She smiled and looked at Cathy. "What happened next?"

Cathy looked around and spotted a nice, shady spot beneath a tree.

"Why don't we sit for this story?" Cathy suggested. Pamela agreed. The women made themselves comfortable beneath the tree.

As they settled down, Cathy began the next part of the story.

# Chapter 5

# Australia

Cathy smiled at the memory as she sat on the long grass, Ellie stretching out beside her. "Several months after I returned from doing the film project my boyfriend and I were taking our dogs for an afternoon walk in May. The air was lovely and the sun was shining…it was a beautiful spring day. The leaves on the trees were beginning to bud, and there was a fresh, newness in the air.

"Behind my home was a vast, open field. Crossing the railway tracks always felt like leaving the town and heading into the country. That day, it felt glorious. We dressed fairly light, tying jackets around our waists, just in case the wind came up or the clouds rolled in.

"The dogs were eager to hit the field. My boyfriend had a big dog. She could have easily passed for a retriever cross, but who knows what she was. She looked tough, but she was a sweet girl. Grabbing onto your wrist and gently poking her teeth into your flesh was her odd sign of her affection for you.

"And of course my dog, Bayleigh—the bichon shih-tzu I had, before Ellie—was with us, with her definite attitude. She always acted more like a cat than a dog. Sometimes we were lucky to get five seconds of affection from her!

"We had the entire day to explore the vast openness of the field. About half an hour away was the Bow River. Oftentimes we would walk along the train tracks, sneak through a barbed wire fence and shimmy down the narrow trail to a path down to the river. Few people knew about it…that's what made it so delicious and adventurous. It was like a scene out of Huck Finn, especially on a warm, spring day.

"The relationship with my boyfriend was relatively new. We had been together just over a year. I loved our adventures. We loved being together. It was magical. We would make love down by the river. We made love everywhere. We had such a passion and a physical connection that we couldn't get enough of each other."

Cathy went on, reminiscing. "We skipped stones as we strolled along the river that day. Soon, the weather started to change. Clouds began to roll in and the temperature changed dramatically. We cut our adventure short and began a brisk walk back home. The wind began to pick up, and as we tried to outrun the weather, it began to snow."

"That's Alberta!" Pamela interrupted.

Cathy shrugged. "Exactly! As we were racing back to the house, I asked jokingly, 'Why the heck do we live here?' My boyfriend replied with a chuckle, 'Yeah, we should move to Australia.' Well. That planted a seed."

"Wait a minute," Pamela sat up for a second. "Don't tell me you moved to Australia because of an offhand comment your boyfriend made on a snowy day in Calgary? Cathy, seriously?!"

Cathy just nodded and continued. "Seriously! That simple thought haunted me for over a year. Throughout the year, I wrestled with it in my mind, over and over." Cathy laughed at the thought. "I actually chewed it to sand. I would ask myself, How is this even possible? Why? What could I possibly do there? I don't even know anything about Australia. I went back and forth: I have to do this! And this is totally irresponsible and whacky. All of these thoughts raced through my mind on a daily basis…yet I couldn't get the thought to go out of my mind. It was a huge leap of faith, and I didn't even know what a leap of faith was! Why was I doing this to myself and what about my family? It was totally crazy."

"Sounds like it, that's for sure," Pamela said.

"When I told my boyfriend I couldn't stop thinking about his comment about moving to Australia, he just said, 'Okay, let's do it!!' Bless his heart, he had no resistance to this crazy idea. Holy crap, I thought. Now I have to follow through!"

"But what about the kids?" Pamela asked.

"Well, next we asked our kids. I had two and he had three. My son was 17 and my daughter was 13. My son was keen. We would wait until he graduated high school and go during his gap year. My daughter was less excited. She would be just entering high school, and her friends were her lifeline.

"My boyfriend's three kids weren't onboard. Since they were a bit older, and at different stages in their lives—either at university or working—they were less likely to join us. Next was my kids' Dad. My son was of legal age to travel; however, I had to get his permission for my daughter to travel and live overseas for a year, since we had joint custody. No resistance there either. Oh no!"

"Oh no?" Pamela asked.

"Oh no, because the more these things lined up, the easier it was to go to Australia, which meant there would be no backing down. I was terrified. It meant we were going.

"And then the going began to feel a lot less scary than not going. Let me rephrase: It seemed more difficult to turn back at that point and not go. Everything was lining up for us to go on this crazy adventure.

"Over the course of the year, I shared with family members and friends about this idea to move to Australia. It was met with mixed reactions. Some people were so excited for us and totally envious. So many people exclaimed how much they wished they could just 'Let go of work, the house, the car, our possessions and just do that!' When I said, 'You can!' they looked at me like I had lost my mind. I wondered if I had!" Cathy chuckled. "They were saying, 'I could never do that. That's too scary to sell everything and strap on a backpack without knowing where you're going to end up in a year.'

"Others had many similar concerns, such as, 'How can give up your careers and be so frivolous? What about your jobs when you get back?'

"That's what I would have asked! That's what I don't even get, now, as I listen to you!" Pamela said.

"Well," Cathy admitted, "I looked at both sides and got very confused. I didn't want to be the irresponsible one, yet I couldn't stop this dream from haunting me.

"It reached a point where I couldn't not go. The feeling was so strong. This really tested my faith in the Universe once again. I still didn't know why this feeling to go was so strong. I just knew I had to trust it."

"Wow, that's a long way to go based on a feeling! And taking the kids…I can't imagine!" Pamela said in awe.

"You know, later, in hindsight, once I knew why I had gone, it made trusting the Universe that much easier," Cathy shrugged.

She went on. "My life coaching course began the day after we arrived in Sydney, and while I was in my course the kids and my boyfriend explored the city and searched for a van to buy. It was our plan to travel around the entire continent, and a van seemed the best way to do it.

"After my coaching training, it was like I had found my passion. I resonated so much with the program and the people in it. I really felt as though this course and the profession had been tailor-made for me. It felt like 'this was it.'

"We set out on our adventure a week or so later in an 8-seater van. We needed eight seats by then as my son had several friends join us. Driving up the coast toward Brisbane was amazing. We hugged the ocean all the way. We explored beaches and little coastal towns and ate PB and J's on the roadside. I was in heaven. I couldn't think of anything more fun than this! With my life coaching course completed, I couldn't wait to start coaching. Shortly afterward I opened my business and started coaching right away with clients back in Canada over Skype. We meandered up the coast. One of our first stops was Byron Bay. Unbelievable. Have you been to Australia?" Cathy asked.

Pamela shook her head, no.

"Well, this little town with all of its quirky folks and shops was magical. And the country embraced us and it began to feel like home. Here was our first real experience of the ocean. We learned to surf and boogie board. Life was very good. We camped for several days before moving up the coast.

"When we hit Brisbane, we all fell in love with the city. It felt like a tropical version of Calgary with the river running through it. It began to heat up, reminding us it most definitely wasn't Calgary. Again, we stayed several days and this time set out to adventure in the city, staying in a hostel rather than camping. It was quite an adventure.

"Before leaving home, we had booked a hotel-type condo just north of Brisbane on the Sunshine Coast in a resort community called Noosa. It became our home for the Christmas season. Our former neighbor introduced us to her sister who lived close by. Knowing someone there, it made sense for us to land for a month or so to enjoy the holidays.

"Christmas wasn't the same in Australia. It's not a big deal there and much less commercial. I suspect it's harder to get excited about a warmly dressed Santa Claus when it's 30+ degrees Fahrenheit. It was so refreshing to not have the pressure. We also thought it would be fun to have shrimp on the barbie, and try kangaroo! We found out that 'shrimp on the barbie' isn't typical Aussie fare; it was just made famous by and old movie, Crocodile Dundee. We thought the kangaroo would be nice and juicy cooked on the barbeque, but it was tough and nasty. What were we thinking?"

"Ha! I would not be keen to try kangaroo." Pamela said, chuckling softly.

"That was the last time we did!" Cathy giggled, and paused briefly. "After Christmas, my son and his friends left for Brisbane to seek fame and fortune, while my daughter stayed with my boyfriend and me. It was our plan to keep moving north up the coast, except I couldn't go. Something in me said, 'You need to stay.' Intuition was still foreign to me, but this pull was really strong. So, I proposed to my daughter and boyfriend that we stay around this area for a while longer. Sure enough, another pebble was dropped and we rented a house right on Sunshine Beach, a great little community. It was perfect. The house was decorated in my favorite turquoise and white colors and had a nautical beach theme. We were right across from several shops and restaurants and the surf club. It was absolutely lovely. We signed a six-month lease. I still couldn't understand why on earth were we staying there!"

"Six months! So I guess you had to start coaching then? How did you guys plan to make money to stay that long?" Pamela asked.

Cathy paused for a minute. "You know, we didn't really worry about it. We had budgeted for a year away, so it really didn't matter where we were in Australia during that year. But I will tell you: The real magic came when I met a group of young women who befriended me quite serendipitously. They called themselves the Goddess Group of Noosa. We would gather and have parties where we would dress up with costumes, feather boas and magic wands; then we would all get into little boats holding candles and twinkle lights while sailing across the little river nearby. It was magical and surreal to be part of this community of women. It felt odd that I was part of this group, yet it felt so natural too. I remember one of the Goddesses saying that there was one more woman who was part of this group, but that she couldn't be part of it physically. She had cancer and was confined to her bed so she wasn't able to attend the events.

"This group of young women, knowing I had just finished my coaching training, asked me if I would coach this woman. Her mind was sharp; however, her body wasn't working well. They felt that if she could heal her body to match her mind she would be able to join our celebrations. So I agreed to see her."

35

"What? You didn't go, did you? You were a coach, not a healer! Who did these women think you were?" Pamela was shocked.

Cathy explained. "That's a good question. I didn't really know what to expect. I began by seeing her once a week for an hour or two at a time. We had deep, rich conversations about every aspect of her life. We eventually started talking about how cancer had affected her life, as well as how her physical ailments aligned with what was going on emotionally – the work of Louise Hay. She was keenly aware of Louise's work and the emotions that may be associated with the cancer. She had done a lot of soul searching and inner work. She was incredibly aware of so many things, and she taught me many things. We continued to have heartfelt conversations over the next several months."

Pamela thought about what she had just heard, but remained silent.

"One day in the middle of our session she declared in her abrupt Aussie manner, 'I'm done.' I said, 'Oh, are you done with coaching?' because I was really hoping that she was not going to say what I thought she was going to say. She said, 'No, I'm done done.'"

Pamela asked, "Like she wanted you to…"

Cathy interrupted gently, "Not quite. I'll explain. After she said that, I immediately wanted to shut it down and say, 'No, no, no. I can't take you there. I'm a life coach,' yet I found myself saying, 'Well, let's explore that.' As soon as I said it, I looked around the room, thinking, "Who said that?" because it scared me, too. There was such magic and power in that conversation that it forever changed our relationship. We had such an incredible bond after that, there was just a knowing. So we explored what that decision would look like for her. I knew it wasn't about me, or what I felt was right for her;

it was about what she wanted and felt was right for her. In listening and in hearing herself, she really could acknowledge that what she was doing was living her life for everyone else, and not for her. She didn't want to disappoint people and she felt, in a way, obligated to be here, for them. She realized in our conversations and over time that she had really done everything she wanted to do, and she was at peace. The fight to beat this disease and to live wasn't her fight. She realized by surrendering to what is was an enormous gift to herself. She was honoring herself by being okay with what life had given her."

Pamela sat, listening, hanging on every word.

"There was so much release and power in her ability to say, 'I choose this. I choose what's going to unfold for me next.' Her struggle was that she did not want cancer to engulf her or swallow her up. She was hanging on because she had been able to control everything and steer her own life in her own direction. Yet, cancer seemed like it was the one that was driving the ship. Our discussion allowed her to see that she could make her own choice – she didn't have to hang on any longer and fight it. She could surrender. Once she made the choice to allow it to just to be, and let her life unfold naturally, it was as if she were throwing a party. She told all of her friends that this was now her decision. She was making a choice. She was choosing how she was going to live the rest of her life.

"It became like planning a party for her. She had arranged to have her casket painted. She wrote her eulogy. She created a poster board with all of her pictures and memories. She recorded her favorite music to be played at the service. She prepared a menu, chose the venue, even picked who was going to read the eulogy. She had all of the elements that she was able to control. She felt like this was the next logical step for her, organically."

"So how did the funeral go?" Pamela wondered.

"I was in awe. It was a beautiful tribute to the woman who became my friend and one of my greatest teachers," Cathy said. "While she was planning this I was traveling in another part of Australia, Tasmania, and she would send me emails sharing what she had accomplished that day. It felt like it really wasn't happening. Still, it was so beautiful as it was unfolding. She was in control of her next step and the journey on which she was about to embark. It was surreal.

"It may have only been five or so weeks from her declaration that day until she passed away. Let me be clear, she did not take her life. She simply made a different choice about how she wanted to live her final days. She got all of those elements in place so that she could surrender to the bigger picture. Letting go of the resistance to what is was really what led her on her beautiful adventure. For the eight years that she'd had cancer, it was like she had been paddling upstream. With her decision she was finally getting in the rowboat and going downstream.

"In her surrender, she found enormous peace and joy. She was able to live her last days exactly as she wanted. She died with a friend reading her poetry, and for her, it was beautiful."

Pamela looked at Cathy thoughtfully. "That is beautiful. I still think I would fight though. I'm so afraid to die."

"Well, I think many people are, but at the same time, there may be a point when we know it's time to surrender. That's what she did. The crazy part of the story, to me, is that in one of our coaching sessions she asked me, 'Why did you come to Australia, Cathy?' I said, 'You know, I really don't know. I just had this really strong pull that I needed to come.' She had the most amazing glint in her eye, and she said, 'I know why you came.' I said, 'Why?' She said, 'Because

I sent for you.' She said, 'You and I were the only ones able to have this conversation. You answered the call, and now you're here.'

"I realized in that moment I absolutely knew she was right. My intuition, another pebble on the path, had guided me there, to that woman, to that conversation and to this relationship that forever changed her life, and mine. I would have never known what I'd have missed had I not gone; had I not trusted my intuition after that snowstorm and in the months that it took me to get to Australia.

"Now that I know, it changes everything. I could have never, ever planned that. I could have never made that story up. It's magical.

"Not only did her choice change her life and the ending of her story, it changed how I saw my role in all of it. I realized how much power there was in coaching...mostly in the listening. I simply became a sounding board so she could hear her own voice. How often do we really hear what each other is saying? She had felt people were talking to her and talking at her, but they really weren't hearing her.

"There's much power in hearing someone and in not assuming what you've heard, but truly hearing what they've said and not trying to fix or to change it in any way. There's so much power in just honoring where they are. That forever changes the person and it forever changes you. I really believe that in a connection or even in a coaching situation, I get just as much from my clients as they get from me. I'm not the one that knows everything. I may be the one who will bring out some wisdom that they already have locked inside of them. How often do we allow that to come out without being afraid of it? How often are we vulnerable enough to express our true feelings without censoring them and with no fear of judgment?

"There are conversations that need to be had that are deeper than the ones we're having. It's about trusting that vulnerability and that intuition, and trusting that whatever you're going to say next is what is meant to be said. Often, we'll use other people as a sounding board so that we can hear ourselves. It's not for anybody else, but for our own good. When we say something out loud, we're forced to acknowledge it and to suddenly know it, and then we cannot un-know what we hear and now know. The seed has been planted, and whether you water it or not, that seed will sprout roots, and it's going to sprout little leaves, and it's going to start to grow. Often we want to stop ourselves when we don't have the answer and we don't have it all figured out. But the true disconnect and the real pain comes when we try to stifle our voice." Cathy trailed off, reflecting.

The women sat in silence before Pamela sat up. "That's an amazing story," she said quietly. "You're so brave; so fearless. I could never have helped that woman the way you did."

"I believe it's in you – it's in all of us," Cathy corrected Pamela gently. "Perhaps right now it's about unstifling your voice. Or letting go of trying to have it all figured out."

"Maybe. I don't even know. Tell me more. I'm enjoying listening to you."

Cathy laughed, "Well, okay. What's the most helpful?"

"All of it!" Pamela said.

## Chapter 6

# Life Speaks

Cathy stroked Ellie's belly and lay down on the grass herself. The sun dappled through the trees and the leaves played in the light breeze. It was so perfect Cathy could not believe the gratitude she was feeling for the nature surrounding them.

She thought for a moment, then went on. "Life speaks to us all day, every day. We bump up against things that don't work that are difficult. People who are difficult; relationships that are challenging. We're stuck in traffic…we get angry at something… There are signs in our life, about our life, and they're usually right in front of us. We don't have to go looking for them. There they are. Like your lump and how you felt this morning when you called me. It's a symptom – it's not the cause."

Pamela sighed, "I'd really like to just run away. It's all too much to deal with."

"But that's just it," Cathy said, "We'd all rather run the other way. We'd rather blame the other person, blame the work, blame the boss, blame the illness…anything rather than look for what it was that actually got us there."

"And what's so wrong with that?"

Cathy laughed, "If we run, we never solve it. And it will keep showing up, in a similar way or different, but I promise you it will show up again. If you ignore the symptom of what this lump in your breast is telling you now, it will keep trying to get your attention. Catch it now, early, and do your inner work. We need to face life in these moments, not run away."

Cathy went on. "As a coach, I would take my clients emotionally spelunking to find what was really at the core of the problem, because it's never about the relationship, the health issue, or the job. It's generally giving us clues about what's going on based on how we're seeing our world. Life mirrors our beliefs and shows us what we need to look at every single day. When we get to the root cause—the belief—we discover that the people in our lives and the challenges we face are really there for us. Not against us. They're messages for us to awaken and to learn from. They're actually gifts—strategically planned gifts I might add—that have come into our lives as a way of helping us move forward. Without adversities and challenges we remain stagnant. Every challenging experience is our teacher." Cathy laughed. "Of course, some teachers are greater than others."

Cathy continued. "Once we go digging and find what that root cause is, the knowledge is profound. With this new perspective, that event or that challenge or that boss or that illness suddenly gives us a greater clarity and wisdom. It gives us greater meaning. It gives us a way to change our lives for the better based on our new vision. Instead of blaming, we take full responsibility for the part we played in it, which unleashes enormous power, direction and courage. We recognize that life isn't happening to us, it's happening for us, which empowers us to make different choices based on what we keep bumping up against over and over and over again.

"Take my story, for instance. Life started whispering to me when I felt unhappy in my job, but I ignored it. So it continued. The whisper became a knock on the door – increased dissatisfaction and feeling like I couldn't fit anywhere anymore. I still pushed through. It took life talking to me by running a big truck through my life—full on divorce and upheaval—before I got the message that I needed to make a change. So it's not about whether or not life will speak to us, because it does, all the time. The question is, how loud does it have to get before we hear the message?"

"Like a lump in my breast, maybe?" Pamela said quietly.

"Do you think it's a whisper?" Cathy asked.

"I hope so. I want to say yes. But I'm worried it's a big truck!"

"Well, if you were to ask your friends if they honestly think you're happy or living a fulfilled life, what would they say? Has it gotten so that you can't quite fake that it's all perfect? Would they say you're at the whisper? They may not even know. And I know you're just starting to make sense of all of this. Are you finding yourself complaining about things like your relationship or your job, or blaming other people and making people bad and wrong in the situation that's challenging you?"

Pamela nodded. "Yes, to all of it." Pamela sighed. "I think I'm past the whisper."

Cathy patted Pamela on the arm. "Good."

43

"Good? What do you mean? None of this is good. I don't want to change my life!"

"Well, most people don't! But when we dig our heels in—when we prevent ourselves from listening to that whisper or that feather—we're only preventing ourselves from moving forward, which is really going with the flow. We're preventing ourselves from just getting in the boat and going downstream. We're working so hard to turn our boat upstream, paddling as fast as we can to get away from the current, trying to control what the challenge or the pain is trying to get our attention about, yet the current—that challenge, that pain—just wants to get us to let go of paddling and go with the flow so we can easily get to where we're really meant to go. Who knows where that current is going to take you, who you're going to meet or what's going to be around the bend in the corner? We think we know, but we don't. Everything we think we need upstream is already waiting for us downstream. Let go of the struggle.

"We feel we need to control life, and it's an illusion when we do. We can't control life! This niggling…this uncomfortable feeling of knowing gets louder and stronger the longer we ignore it. Can you imagine what life would be like if we were always in the boat going downstream, accepting what comes our way, enjoying the view and the scenery, allowing life to unfold without needing to control it? Feeling like we have an innate sense that we're safe and knowing that what's coming our way is the best for us? Having no clue what's around the bend yet trusting completely that every time we let go of control and allow ourselves to freefall into this place of unknowing, there's something even more magnificent around the corner than we could ever imagine?!" Cathy stood up and shook the grass off her legs. She helped Pamela stand up.

"Come on. Let's get to the top of the hill." Cathy called out for Ellie, who came bounding out of the nearby meadow, ready to walk with the women again.

"I can't imagine," Pamela said as they began walking.

"Do you really think we can figure it all out?"

"Yes, I do. I figure it out all day every day for my family. I figure it out for my work. I am a CFO, for goodness' sake! I solve problems all day. Why is it so difficult just to solve my own happiness?"

"What do you need to do to let go of being in control of everything?"

Pamela shrugged. "I can't just let go. I can't just fall. Maybe you can work in a coffeeshop but I can't. I just can't."

Cathy explained, "Imagine a monkey in a tree, swinging from branch to branch. The monkey has to actually let go of one of the branches in order to grab another. Now imagine you're the monkey holding of one of the branches. The branch is your office – your high-level stress. You want to make a change so you go to reach the branch over there, and as you're swinging there's a moment of suspension, of letting go and of feeling like there's nothing below you. You've just let go of the security of the first branch on one side, and you don't know if the branch on the other side will support you or what it's going to be like, while down below there's a cavern – a huge, vast space of unknowingness.

"This uncertainty scares the heck out of us! Yet, if we don't let go of the first branch before we grab the second, we get caught between two branches—two decisions—and then what do we do? Let go? We're no longer in motion. So do we dangle? We're suspended in midair, feeling like we've got control when we're really just hanging on for dear life. This prevents the natural flow of events and of life, and stops us from just going down the river. It's like we're paddling upstream and not getting anywhere. We stop the process of life. This may be why so many people feel stuck and uninspired. This dangling feels more uncomfortable than the ease of swinging from branch to branch!"

"Except that I don't even have a second branch. And I'm not swinging. I'm the one hanging onto my branch for dear life!"

Cathy laughed, "Aha, so you DO see the situation you're in. Now, do you see how there is a natural rhythm? It's like a pendulum. When we hold on to one branch, we stop the pendulum. And when we hold on to both branches at the same time because we're fearful of letting go, we also stop the pendulum. It stops that flow.

"In the story I shared with you a moment ago about my career, I knew I was hearing the whisper and the feather and the two-by-four, I just wasn't willing to let go of the branch. I was afraid. I couldn't let go because being in midair meant uncertainty. I didn't know what was next. I wanted to know what was next. I wanted certainty. I wanted to know what career I was going to next before I let go, so I stayed. Much too long.

"I had to reach the end of my rope to actually break free. The rope had to break away before I could allow myself to freefall. I still didn't know what was next at the time, but I was in a place where I had to let go of one branch or the other. This gave me a vast opportunity to explore my future, knowing that I still had skills and tools to draw on. I was just trusting that another branch would appear, and it did."

Pamela shook her head. "This makes no sense. Why would we choose this? I have everything I could want. I have a beautiful home, husband, children, and a six-figure salary. Why would I let go of anything? And trust? Trust what? I don't know, Cathy. I just don't think I'm cut out for this new way of thinking."

"Yes, I get. This isn't new, it's just new to you. Trusting that flow and the universe takes time and patience, and lots of practice. But my friend, as you begin to trust yourself, and this flow, the universe will always support you. It will always bring you to a place of feeling safe and secure, knowing something magnificent is just around the corner. When we trust and believe there's something greater than us truly taking care of us, despite the unknowing, miracles unfold in our lives that we could have never predicted. People show up in our lives that help us create that new business; doors open that were once closed; we find love in the most unimaginable place. That something greater is really all-knowing and all-trusting and will give us what we need when we need it. Not on our time, but on divine time, when we're really ready for it – when we're actively doing our own inner work in order to get us to the next place, whatever that looks like."

"Oh. Like religion? I go to church once in a while."

Cathy shook her head, "No, not necessarily religion. Just the faith that there is something more to us and to the world. A belief that everything along our path is providing us the opportunity to grow and discover the next piece that's ready for us that's part of our calling; that's part of our purpose for being on this planet.

"When we hold back and don't allow the flow of events to happen, we prevent the gifts from reaching us in a timely manner. We prevent things from naturally occurring as they're meant to. I would often ask my clients, 'Who do we think we are that we know better than the universe, or spirit or the divine? Who do we think we are, believing we know more than the creator, what's best for us, our lives, our neighbor, or the good of the planet? That we know the divine plan or we can see the bigger picture?' If we were to surrender to the all-knowing and all-great, and put our trust into the project manager—the one who always has our back and will take care of us—we'd be allowing things to unfold in a way that's magnificent and in alignment with everything in this world that's meant to be. We're really just a part of the bigger picture that's unfolding at exactly the perfect moment." Cathy paused. "How do you know something's perfect Pamela?"

Pamela thought for a moment, then shrugged. "You know what? I have no idea!"

"Because it's happening right now. That's all we need to know. Life is perfectly orchestrated for our highest good."

Pamela stopped on the trail. They were at the base of a foothill, and a steep climb was ahead. "I have to believe there is a God first, then?"

Cathy stopped beside Pamela and they both looked up at the foothill. "Not necessarily." She smiled as she got an idea. "But by the time we get to the top of this hill, I have a hunch you'll be ready to start listening to your intuition."

Pamela laughed and said, "Okay, now you're starting to sound like Oprah."

"Hey, now there's a wise woman!" Cathy said. "Let's go!" Cathy started up the steep trail, Ellie at her feet. Pamela fell into step right behind.

# Chapter 7

# To the Hilltop

"Okay, so I don't really know what intuition is. But how do you think you'll make me believe in following mine so quickly?"

"Oh, let's just see what shows up." Cathy watched as Ellie took off ahead up the trail. "In my experience working with people, I've found that many of them want to override their intuition. They don't want to trust those feelings – those little thoughts or nigglings that just come up. They want to ignore them because they're foreign and they're scary. They don't actually believe they can trust that voice. Something tells them that if they follow it, they might actually have to take a different action than they're used to. And that can be really scary.

"Of course, when it comes to intuition, often the action makes no sense at all. We want clarity. We want to make sense of everything. We want to have control – at least we want to feel we have a sense of control over the situation or the action that's required. We're used to defaulting to what's familiar. It might not be comfortable or get us the desired outcome, however it's something that we're used to and that we can get our hands on. And that makes us feel safe, and makes life feel safe. But in the end, it really doesn't get us heading in the right direction. It keeps us stuck and going around in circles. And we wonder why we keep attracting the same kind of people and situations time and time again. I've been there. Too many times to count. I'm sure you've heard the definition of insanity?

"Oh yeah…" Pamela said.

In unison, Pamela and Cathy said, "…Doing the same thing over and over again and expecting different results." They laughed.

Cathy went on. "Really, though, few of us know how to trust our intuition. We've been taught to override it and go with our head more than our hearts because it feels so uncomfortable to go with your heart. Your head is more logical. The brain cannot understand when you go with something that just feels right. It just doesn't make any sense. As a society we just keep plugging along, running just as fast as we can away from what our heart tells us. We listen to what our brains tell us to do, which is generally based on what society deems is right – all of the "shoulds" that we have collectively agreed upon and believe are right. We overlook what our gut is trying to tell us, what our intuition is trying to guide us toward, the things that don't feel right, the things that aren't working, the job that we don't like, the relationship that starts to go a little bit south, and we turn right instead of left. We we think we know better and can outsmart our gut feelings.

"It never fails that when we override our intuition, things usually don't work as well as they could. We find ourselves heading towards more roadblocks. Doors seem to close rather than open when we ignore our spidey-senses. It somehow feels wrong to want to trust your intuition."

"Well, I mean, come on! I don't know about you but people who just wander around trusting their intuition…they're not thinking logically. Seriously, I could never…" Pamela interjected.

Cathy continued anyway. "When we do trust our intuition, however, the doors start to open. Magic starts to happen and the miracles begin to unfold. You know those coincidences or happenstance moments that cannot be explained? Someone calls shortly after you were thinking of them? An opportunity suddenly lands in your lap that wasn't there before? Often those moments scare us even more than the painful feeling of being stuck or in a place we don't want to be because they're unfamiliar and uncharted territory. We'll often go down the path of least resistance because it's what we know. Well-meaning people in our lives have convinced us it's the right way. We listen to these people, despite a deep knowing that it's not right for us, that it's not the right way. All the same, we still continue down that path even though it doesn't feel right. There's that uncomfortable feeling of knowing that there's something more – that there's something juicier on the other side. We're so afraid to step outside of the box that we'll stay inside by choice and feel like we're trapped. We see that the door or the window is open, and we won't necessarily want to go through it. Plus, many of our friends and people that we know are in the box with us. It feels uncomfortably comfortable. Uncomfortably numb, as the song says. We've put the lid on our own box. But we can also remove it."

"Wow, that really resonates with me," Pamela interjected. "It does feel uncomfortably comfortable. But I'm doing all the right things.

I do what everyone else does and expects me to do. I have a house, and kids, and a car, and I go shopping on Saturdays. I'm doing everything right, but I'm still not happy. I thought these things made you happy! What's wrong with me? Do I need a bigger house? A better job?"

"That's just it. Things don't bring happiness. See, you're starting to get that being in the box doesn't feel comfortable anymore. If you made the decision right now to start trusting your intuition in every choice and decision in your life, and you could see your life through a crystal ball, you wouldn't even recognize it, or yourself, because what you think you want in your life now and how you've mapped and planned it all out will look nothing like the life your intuition sees and actually has in store for you. It would completely blow your mind to see where you will be in that two weeks, two months, five years or ten years if you followed your intuition. As much as we think we're in control of our life, and yes, we are when we're being present from moment to moment, there is so much more that is trying to come through us. We're here to contribute our natural talents in a significant way to the world, and that is suffocated when we keep ourselves trapped inside of the box.

"I see more and more people realizing that this old way of looking at life is no longer working for them. People who are coming out of the box are contributing in ways that align with who they are and what they're meant to do. As a result their lives are full of more happiness and joy. They're contributing in a more natural, organic way than they ever thought possible. There is a great Joseph Campbell quote that says 'You must give up the life you planned in order to have the life that is waiting for you,' and it's spot-on. There is a life that is waiting for you that aligns with who you are, the whole world and the whole universe. I know that's a lot to grasp; however, life conspires to give you more of what's good for you and everyone on the planet. With that comes a sense of joy and peace and harmony. The hard part is trusting and being in a place where you can say, 'I'm going to trust something that isn't tangible, that I can't touch or smell, that I can only feel, and I'm going to completely let go and freefall.'" Cathy giggled. "You feel it in here, with your whole heart. You feel it with your body. But you can't make sense of it. Explaining to someone why you sell everything and move to Australia on a gut feeling is most often met with a big 'Are you crazy!?' People want something concrete. People want to have something tangible. They want to know why and how. When you don't know that, it's hard to explain. You may seem like you're flaky or you're whimsical or you're irresponsible, because we've been taught to be responsible. You even question yourself, often!"

Pamela said, "Yeah, like you said before. It's the trust part that I still don't think I get. And what if my intuition is wrong?"

"Good question! Your intuition is never, ever wrong. It just may take you in completely different directions than you could have imagined, or how you thought something would look or turn out. When you sign onto trusting your intuition you start this amazing magical, mystery tour of life. You can't access it if you're not open and listening. If you ignore your intuition, however, and you stay in the box, you will likely feel trapped. You may feel like you're missing something. And you'll probably get into a place emotionally where you're feeling sad or depressed, and feeling like people have figured it out and you're the only one who hasn't. There may be a sense of longing, or trapped energy that has nowhere to go because it's confined within a box. Once you step out of the box, you see that there is this whole world that you had access to and you didn't even know it was available to you. That can be even scarier than staying in the box. Quite often what happens is people will take a little peek to see what's out there but they will come back into the box because they're afraid of this big, vast, amazing experience and world that they never allow themselves to explore. That can be even more daunting than staying in a box where you're confined."

Pamela stopped to catch her breath. "Ah, it's steep, Cathy!"

Cathy paused a little ways ahead and took a few deep breaths herself. "It's good though. A challenge. Yes?"

Pamela regulated her breathing, and asked, "But how exactly do I get out of the box? Does this really have to happen now?"

"How much longer are you prepared to feel unhappy? What if this lump is truly a gift in your life? What if it's an opportunity to live more in alignment with your true self and your soul? What if this is the wake-up call that we hear so many people talk about – a second chance? What's holding you back from making a change?" Cathy shrugged.

Pamela thought about it for a moment. "I don't know, Cathy."

"Let's keep going. Maybe you're not ready, and that's okay. When I had my wake-up call, it was like I had no choice. It had to happen. Maybe you're not there yet?"

Pamela shrugged as she continued along the steep path. "I don't even know 'where' I am."

Cathy followed behind Pamela, walking slowly and steadily, keeping her breath deep and even. "Ah. Maybe it's time I talked about letting go of who you aren't."

# Chapter 8

# Letting Go of Who You Aren't

As they hiked, Cathy explained, "If you really want to crack open the box you may want to consider letting go of who you aren't."

"Huh? What do you mean?" Pamela quizzed.

"Over the course of our lives we put on masks—layers of them—and build walls to protect us. We wear masks so we can be who other people want us to be. I remember for my 40th birthday party, my husband threw me a surprise party. All of my friends and family were there. I panicked. I didn't know who to be in a group of people who I wore different masks around. I was one way with my childhood friends, another with my community, and another with my film community. It was the first time I realized that I was nothing to myself, and I didn't actually know who I was. After that, I slowly began to shed the masks, one at a time. It wasn't easy, and I felt exposed. I totally wanted to hide behind those different masks to be safe, yet I could no longer trick myself into being something I wasn't. It's so much easier to live without masks. When you're true to yourself, people either take you or leave you. But in the end you're the only person you must face every day.

"We put up facades that shape and mold us into being something that we're not, yet everything to everyone. It's exhausting. I wanted to run out of my party screaming because I didn't know who to be.

"We become chameleons of sorts, trying to fit in and trying to be loved and accepted. The whole time, we've only been deceiving ourselves. And I really believe people know when we're not being authentic. Ultimately we then attract people to us who are also wearing their false self.

"Eventually the rubber hits the road, and there is great discomfort and anxiety, because we innately know that we've sold out and have sold our soul in order to fit in, to be what we think people want us to be, to be like everyone else and to basically not upset the apple cart. We're all in the same boat.

"I would argue that we were taught that in school and in the general structures that our society is built upon. This wanting to be like somebody else is really a deep desire to be accepted and to fit in. We all want to feel like we belong and that we matter. If we don't feel we matter, then we'll look for validation externally, through someone else's eyes. So, we try to mold and shape ourselves to be that person that everyone likes, to feel that validation. No wonder we have anxiety! And it's excruciating – we're trying to squeeze into 'skin' that doesn't fit!"

"Tell me about it," Pamela said under her breath.

"We don't even really recognize who we are because we've molded our lives to fit some ideal that looks perfect on the outside, but is a mess on the inside. I know for myself, I created a life where everything looked like I had it all figured out. I had a great career. I had a great husband. I had a great family. I had a dog. I had a big house. I had great friends.

"I had it all, yet nothing fit. I was empty and unhappy. I had created a perfect life to match everyone else's ideals. Nothing fit me. I started taking off the masks. I was taking off the old skin – the protective armor. Shaking things up. I took off the suit that no longer fit. It was a time in my life when I wasn't popular with those around me. People around me didn't want me to change. To take off those masks discard the façade. It meant they may have also have to stop pretending. They, too, weren't being true to themselves.

"I had to get completely naked. It was a very difficult time.

"I was never truer to myself than when I took off all of that extra baggage that I had carried around that I thought I had to wear. I was raw, and I was exposed. Honestly, I didn't know who I was. I didn't know at the end of the day who Cathy was. That was the scariest thing ever – to see myself in this vulnerable state of nothingness. It was like the bottom dropped out. I couldn't find my clothes. I couldn't grab onto anything that felt familiar or safe. I knew nothing for certain. What I realized was that I had to build who I was from the ground up, based on who I really was – not who I thought I should be, but who I truly was. That sense of freedom and that sense of willingness to show up in my vulnerability and in my uncertainty was the best gift I could have given myself. This is what began the next journey into myself."

She turned to Pamela. "So I ask you, with Daryl, do you feel like you can show up as yourself?"

57

Pamela nodded. "I think so. I think I do."

Cathy asked, "Well, let me ask you this. Are you authentic in that relationship?"

Pamela thought for a moment. "Well, I don't like him to see me without makeup. I definitely feel the pressure to keep the house clean and always have dinner ready on time for him. I…sometimes I don't tell him…everything."

"So are you still in that feeling of wanting him to see only your best and you don't really show him all the stuff underneath because that might scare him away? I can say that for me, I told you about the wake-up call I had in my 40's, but I recognized it again, even more recently in my 50's. It's another unraveling of who I am not, and I don't think I'm alone in this. I always took the best pieces of myself and that's who I revealed in my relationship, and in fairness to the other person they never really saw who I was. I'm a giver, and I gave freely and didn't ask of others. Always being the giver and not asking in return was the pattern I created in all my relationships. I put aside my needs and gave what I thought he needed.

"I wanted so much to be loved and to be accepted, that I completely ignored myself and my values. I ignored many red flags, which I've since recognized was slowly eroding my self-worth. I kept making excuses for why I couldn't take action and I was afraid of trusting myself, all the while knowing that things didn't feel right yet I was so afraid to address it. I was terrified of making a change – I didn't want another failed relationship. What would that have said about me? Yet I knew by speaking my truth and standing up for me and what I valued that everything would change, again. And it did. Life put me up against a wall where I had to choose: Stay stifled and put the other person's feelings and values first, or stand up for what mattered most to me and speak my truth. Another layer of my true self had been revealed, which ultimately left me feeling raw and vulnerable. How do you stand up for your truth after you've been trying to be someone else the whole time?

"I tried anyway, and once I started talking about it and making waves it was really difficult, because I was revealing another side of myself that I had never revealed in my relationship before. It was hard stuff for both of us. I'm sure he felt blindsided. Yet I knew I had to put myself first – my real, whole, messy self. The authentic me. She had to come out. It seemed like I was making a terrible mistake at the time, however I realized that a mistake is only a mistake if you don't learn from it. I can certainly say, I learned a powerful lesson from this, one that I am so grateful for now, even though I still feel the sting of it as I share it with you now. Being that honest with myself about myself was an enormous gift. Hiding behind who I felt I needed to be to save the relationship wasn't fair to either one of us. Feeling I was protecting him prevented me from standing in my truth. In reality I was really protecting myself from being the one to shake things up."

"Hmmm." Pamela said. Cathy knew that meant she could relate. Pamela didn't offer anything, but the wheels were clearly turning in her mind.

Cathy went on, "I also know that quite often what we do is anticipate that after a certain amount of time with someone, or if we marry someone, we believe we're going to change them, or that this person will want to change and be who we want them to be."

"Oh yes, I know. I felt that way. I totally wanted to change Daryl." Pamela interjected.

"And? Have you?"

"Oh, how I've tried, but no!"

"Exactly. Because what you see is what you get. Quite often we as women go in naïve, expecting more, seeing the best in someone yet not seeing the actual picture of who they are. I speak from experience – I saw something in him that he didn't or couldn't see in himself. The more I encouraged him to be who I saw, the more he dug his heels in resisting the change. Who was I to want to change him, anyway? Yet I believed at some level that I could change him or even save him from himself. He didn't believe he needed to be changed or saved. In fact, in the end he was perfectly content to be who he was. Who did I think I was to think I knew better than he did? What had happened was my perspective changed, and I could no longer ignore the feeling of discontent, another feather, or another two-by-four. Signs had been there all along, yet I wasn't seeing them or the whole picture. I had only been seeing parts and ignoring the rest. Once I saw the big picture I knew I had to speak up. I could no longer silence my voice.

"I realized I was turning myself into a pretzel trying to be something I wasn't and trying to fit into his world and adopt his values versus upholding mine. I gave so much of myself away. In trying to save someone else, I sold out on myself. I had very few boundaries and the ones I did have I allowed to be compromised."

Cathy stopped on the trail and looked at Pamela as she said. "You know, I really think my body is trying to tell me something." She stopped beside Cathy, who was happy for a chance to catch her breath.

"How do you know?" Cathy asked.

"Because it just hit me," Pamela said. "Just as you were telling that story. I suddenly didn't feel good. That's so weird."

"Interesting," Cathy said. "That's just what I was going to share with you – how playing someone else to please him, and especially not valuing my standards and setting boundaries, was making me physically ill."

"Oh? That is interesting! In what way?"

"My gosh, in a huge way!" Cathy exclaimed. She could feel a deeper insight ready to be found, despite having processed all of this several times over. "Pamela, I didn't sleep well for over four years. Four years!"

"Wow," Pamela said. "No wonder you didn't feel good."

"I know, right? Our sleep has a lot to tell us. If you have something going on and you're ignoring it your body will often wake you up. I think the universe was giving me a strong message. I kept wanting to fix it with herbal remedies or various things; however, in the end, once I made the decision to be true to me, I started sleeping like a baby."

"Really?" Pamela said, surprised. "Just like that?"

"Yes!"

"I have to admit, I'm having difficulty sleeping. I just thought I worried a lot." Pamela said.

Cathy asked, "What do you think is keeping you awake?"

Pamela didn't answer right away. "I feel a lot of resentment with my job and maybe with Daryl. I get angry with him a lot, although I try never to let it show. I just swallow it and pretend everything is okay. Same with my job, but I really resent all the time and energy it takes…especially that it takes me away from my family. My kids. I worry about my kids. I never have a minute to myself."

Pamela paused thoughtfully, "You know, Cathy," she began, "I'm not convinced my emotions have anything to do with my health.

It's probably genetic. My grandmother had breast cancer. It's just something happening in my body."

Cathy looked at her friend. She knew she had sparked that reaction. She decided to ease off on talking about the connection, although she knew this health issue was scaring Pamela. She knew, too, that her reaction was only inviting her to explore something deeper with her.

"Well, perhaps you're right," Cathy offered. "Still, aligning with our values is a very powerful way to live, and I'm not convinced many of us are living this way. My strongest values are my family, trust and connection. When I'm in a situation, or when I'm faced with an opportunity and I'm not sure what to do, I'll ask myself, 'Does this align with my family? Is this something or someone I can trust? Do I have a strong connection to this person or experience?' As well, I'll ask myself, 'Is this for my highest good?' Our values define who we are; they're the touchstone by which we live. I know when I'm not living aligned with my values, things don't feel right, and I start to feel out of balance and disconnected from myself.

"When you try to live someone else's values you dishonor yourself, which in turns causes stress and anxiety. Being out of sync with our values keeps us up at night. It may seem to serve a relationship for a period of time but in the end it doesn't work for either person. My relationship began to deteriorate with the resentment, bitterness and anger I was feeling, especially around my number two value, trust. In any relationship, personal or business, if you don't have trust what do you have?

"I love something my friend and colleague, Danielle Reed, who created values cards called What Matters: A way for families to have powerful conversations about values while at the dinner table, said:

'Values are what matter most to us. They're an internal compass guiding us to be who we truly are.'"

Pamela was quiet as Cathy shared. After a while, she finally said, "I'm not living aligned with my values. I can relate to yours – they're mine too. And I don't know if Daryl is either." She leaned on a tree. They were nearing the top of the hill, and it was getting steeper. "Whew. That was hard to say."

"Welcome to AFGO!" Cathy said with a smile.

"A-?" Pamela asked.

"Another frickin' growth opportunity. One of my friends reminds me of this all the time – that they're all around us. And they especially show up when people come into our lives to mirror behaviors, patterns or limitations in our life. Blind spots – we all have them. Other people may see our blind spots. Some may even point them out. When they do, we often want to ignore them, run away and do almost anything to distract ourselves from doing the work we need to do to eliminate them. It's work. Hard, painful, gut-wrenching work. It's easier to move across the country than to face them. You may be able to run from your challenges, from people you don't like or from a circumstance that tests your patience, but you can't hide from it forever. The gifts will keep showing up again and again, with someone else mirroring that same behavior to us, for us. We may blame others for the fact that we're being treated in a certain way and point fingers at the same type of person showing up time and time again in our lives: An abusive romantic relationship, a condescending boss, a rude clerk, a gossiping, judging friend. They keep showing up. They're different, but the same."

"You know, you're right!" Pamela said as she continued up the steep trail. "I have this colleague, and she drives me nuts. And when

63

I think about it, she is exactly like my mother-in-law! They even look similar. Huh."

"Talk about patterns!" Cathy said. "Challenging relationships are our greatest gifts. People are in our lives for a reason…they're bringing us a gift. Wrapped in a bright red bow."

"Some bow – like how they both nitpick and criticize me every single time we interact?"

"Yes. I had a friend who was never able to tell me the truth. She was constantly lying to me, while I valued truth and honesty. Of course, I had to look at this as a reflection of how was I not able to tell myself the truth. I had to ask, was I lying to myself in some way? We have to look at these reflections as learning opportunities. Otherwise, it's just frustrating and we just write people off. So, how do you nitpick and criticize others? Or, maybe more accurate, how do you nitpick and criticize yourself?"

"UGH! That's way too deep for me."

Cathy laughed. "Yes it is, and yet it can be freedom when you see it. Years ago, when I opened that Pandora's box and begrudgingly looked inside, I discovered it was pretty full. For instance, when I told myself I would do something, and then didn't, dozens of times throughout the day, I wasn't being truthful. It was simple things, like planning to leave the house a bit early to ensure I was calmly on time for an appointment, and then leaving late and having to race thru traffic, ending up feeling anything but calm once I arrived. It was the times I'd plan to exercise, and didn't, leaving me feeling sluggish and unmotivated all day; the times I'd promise myself I would have a salad at lunch and instead have a pizza; the times I didn't go to bed early so I wouldn't be tired the next day; the times I didn't go for a walk, or make a necessary phone call and miss an opportunity…it went on and on.

"Interestingly, once I began to look at those little white lies I told myself and began to clean each one of them up, I found that my friend—the one who was lying to me—rarely did anymore. It was profound. Life speaks to us by bringing people and events into our lives that may mirror our behavior in the same way or in a similar way to show us what we need to look at. And if we're willing to see that person as that mirror we can learn so much from them. It may be a negative behavior or pattern that we need change – one that we keep bumping up against, time and time again. Each time, the mirror becomes larger, and more clear. As the messages become stronger and more magnified, it becomes time to consider looking at the mirror. Annoying people or situations are simply a way to change or alter something that may be holding us back in our own life. Mirror, mirror."

"Hmmm," Pamela said. "Except I don't see how I nitpick them, or me…"

"Take a closer look. We all have people who don't treat us with respect, or are maybe even abusive. What is that telling us? How are we not respectful of ourselves? Do we honor our self-promises? And I'm talking about something as simple as not honoring the promise to eat better and exercise more, or finishing the book for next week's book club. Or it could be the promise you made to finish that baby blanket – and now that baby is a toddler. On and on it goes. These catch up with us over time and chip away at our self-worth and self-trust. That's huge. If we don't have trust in ourselves to do what we say, who can we trust?

"I recently read Iyanla Vanzant's book Trusted. In it there was a quote by someone that was profound and really struck me: 'To be trusted is a greater compliment than being loved.'"

"Wow! That's huge." Pamela said. She processed that for a moment before speaking. "I think I trust myself. I don't know. It makes me think of this gossiping, judging friend of mine who once got up in the middle of dinner and walked out after telling me all the reasons why I was not a good friend to her, and how I really should behave in order to be her friend. Is there a gift in that?" Pamela asked.

Cathy responded, "Painfully, yes. How does that show up in your life, or more accurately, in the relationship you have, or don't have, with you? Gossiping and judging others – ugly but true. Are you judging others? And are you judging yourself? Maybe you're oversharing stories about yourself with people who haven't earned the right to hear them and to hold them in their confidence. Or sharing other people's stories when you really should be holding them sacred in a vault. Author, Brené Brown speaks of this in her book Daring Greatly. Is there a mirror there for you?"

Pamela groaned. "I don't think so. I don't do any of that. I don't gossip and judge the way those friends do."

Cathy tilted her head and looked slyly at Pamela, "You sure about that? That may be true; however, are you prepared to invite another person or adversity to come into your life to teach you? I think the question becomes, 'At what point do you want to look at this unpleasant situation as a gift?' Because it will come back again if you don't get it this time around, and it will be a much stronger mirror – a magnifying glass." Cathy laughed.

"Oh I don't want that! It's like those really annoying clients I have, I guess." Pamela said. "Or even my kids, when they're acting up."

"Oh, don't get me started on the gifts from our children!" Cathy laughed. Ellie ran up to her at the sound of her laughter. "They were my greatest teachers when they were growing up! I wish I had paid more attention back then; I'd have had it all figured out by now," Cathy said before bursting into laughter once more.

"What about those people bearing gifts – do we still need to be in a relationship with them…the ones who bring me those delicious gifts as you call them?"

Cathy answered. "The answer is yes and no. These people are in your life for a reason. They're either there for this lesson, or they're in your life for a season or a lifetime. You get to choose. Like my children – they're in my life for a lifetime. Some friends are in my life for a season, and others for a reason. Listen to your gut or what your heart is telling you. You'll know how it feels to be with them. If you're not meant to keep them in your life, thank them energetically or physically for their gift, and gracefully send them away. If they are meant to be in your life, thank them and give them a great big hug. They stuck it out to show you the way to yourself. Trust that you'll know when you know. The ebbs and flows of all of the relationships in our life are magnificent gifts, that provide us with new self-discoveries and life lessons. Listen to your heart; it will show you the way."

Both women laughed. Pamela started hiking again. "But wait, you said that by the time we reach the top of the hill, you'd have me believing in my intuition. We've only talked about values and relationships."

Cathy shrugged. "Well, you know, I suppose we have to follow the ebb and flow even in our conversations. I promise, intuition is coming. I have some good stories for you!" She scanned the rest of the trail ahead. "Looks like we're getting close, though!"

The women continued up the steep trail, listening to the birds. Cathy could tell by Pamela's body language that she was more relaxed than when they began, and she wondered if Pamela had yet heard what she needed to from her.

# Chapter 9

# The Gift of Your Intuition

They reached the top of the foothill and were rewarded with a remarkable view of the mountains on one side and the valley they had come up from on the other. Pamela found a shady spot by a tree, and stretched out her legs before sitting beneath it.

Cathy followed suit, bending forward to stretch her hamstrings a bit. Both women were winded, flushed and smiling.

"So now. Intuition?"

"Ah, yes. My favorite thing!" Cathy laughed. "Of course, I didn't always know what intuition was. It simply kept knocking on my door, trying to get my attention, until I couldn't ignore it any longer. I had to pay attention to it. I also couldn't explain it, and many times it didn't make any sense. Things just started happening that were too much of a coincidence. I think they were always happening, I just wasn't ready to listen. Oftentimes, I would get a niggling or a feeling in my gut, and I didn't really know what to do with it. It would tell me to go into a store I didn't usually go into. One day it strongly nudged me to go to a local coffee shop before I had even had my morning shower. I fought the thought, and then remembering how intuition speaks to us, surrendered. When I would trust that feeling and do what it asked, I was always amazed what was there for me. This particular time, a friend who I hadn't seen in a very long time was there at that coffee shop. After we talked for a bit she offered me a solution to a problem I had no answer to. I walked away astounded and delighted. Our intuition speaks to us each and every moment of the day.

"My intuition speaks to me all the time in forms of feeling. Generally, I get a feeling or I get shivers. I call them 'cha-chings.' So, when I've got something that I'm going to do I or ask the universe for a sign, my intuition will either just leave me alone or will give me a cha-ching. That's when I get goosebumps and tingling all over my body. I know with every fiber of my being that the universe is supporting me at that moment to move forward with an idea or take action via my intuition, and I know that it's the right way to go. When I don't listen to my intuition, things don't work. Things don't align. I start bumping up against walls. I find challenges. When I listen to my intuition, things really start to flow, and flow smoothly. It's not that there aren't challenges along the way—that's different—but there's a fluidity and acceptance of the process.

"It's important to trust your intuition. Trusting your intuition moves you in the direction that your soul wants you to go, for your highest and best good. And with that the universe will support you, every step of the way. I've had many clients who don't want to believe in their intuition. They're afraid of it. We have been taught to listen to our mind and to let it guide us through our life. Our brain can tell us logically what to do. We want to be able to control or sort something out in a way that seems logical based on our ticker-tape minds – this is what's going to happen and these are the steps of how it's going to happen. How often do we talk ourselves out of great ideas because we can't figure out the next logical step, so we dismiss them? Yet what if that's the path of least resistance, and once you take that first step, the rest of the path will reveal itself as stepping stones? Martin Luther King said, 'Take the first step in faith. You don't have to see the whole staircase – just take the first step.'

"We can't fathom the idea of getting a strong impression to move to Australia. 'What's that about?' That scares the crap out of us. 'Where did that come from?' Yet you know, once you have a thought or once your intuition nudges you, you can't un-know it. Usually you can't stop thinking about it. It's like a haunting. It won't ever go away until you pay attention to it. No matter how hard you try, no matter how much you drink, how far you run – you cannot run away from it. Have you had any thoughts like that?"

Pamela opened her eyes and replied, "Um. Maybe?"

"Like…?" Cathy asked.

Pamela sighed. "Okay, I have definitely had the thought, more than once, that it's time to quit my job. I've been curious about taking a pottery class. But that can't be my intuition…That's just boredom, I think."

Cathy suggested, "Could that simple thought—that curiosity—be your intuition speaking to you? Wanting you to follow it? It doesn't mean you have to quit your job and buy a pottery studio, but why not take one small step and inquire about a pottery class? What have you got to lose? See how it feels when you get there. You may meet some interesting people.

"When I got the nudge, or the shove I should say, to go to Australia, had I not listened to my intuition—had I numbed myself out—I would never have known what I missed. Thankfully, I did listen, and enjoyed the profound experience that was awaiting me. I had no idea at the time how life-changing making that simple yet complex decision to go would be, or just how significant a part it played in shaping the next part of my life. It completely changed how I saw my life, how I coached my clients and eventually how I lived my life, all because I trusted my intuition that one time. I began to trust my gut, more and more. It was something that I didn't even know I had access to before. And my life kept getting better and better. The people I would meet; the amazing experiences I would have; it led to opportunities I could have never imagined. All because of a single choice of trusting something unknown and completely foreign. The logical mind wants to make sense of things and makes things bad and wrong. By trusting my gut, I now know I will always be taken care of. Something greater than me has my back. I always know that the experience that I'm meant to have is the next step on my journey. And, the more you learn to trust your gut, the more fun you can have with it."

"Huh? How is that?" Pamela asked curiously.

"Really! The more you trust your intuition, the more you can play with it a bit and begin to ask it for signs. You can ask to be shown the answers. This is where I have all kinds of stories – and you may not believe them, but they're all true! Over my years in coaching I often asked my clients to use this technique to help their unfolding paths be revealed."

"Okay, so what's the technique?" Pamela wanted to know.

"Let me explain. I had a client several years ago who felt she wanted to move to Australia. She had a very strong feeling. She was living in Canada at the time, just like me, in fact! She had wanted to move to Australia for over half her life. She kept getting a feather… and then a whisper…and she kept digging her heels in and denying the messages and fighting the feeling. Then once it became so loud and so strong—when it was a two-by-four—I made a request of her. I simply asked, 'What if you just looked for a sign? What if you play with this a little bit and see where it will take you?' She asked what I meant, and I told her that whenever I was stuck on a decision, I would ask the universe—the project manager—to give me a sign or to point me in the right direction."

"Come on, Cathy. Really? A sign? Now you're sounding a little too woo-woo." Pamela exclaimed.

"Hey, take it or leave it!" Cathy laughed. Then she teased lightly with a smile, "But listen through to the end of the story!" She paused for a moment to let her friend reconnect to what she was saying. "In saying this to my client, I offered up the ability for her to be able to think of something on the fly and give herself an end time and then to allow the universe to take care of her. She, of course, was also apprehensive at first. She wanted to trust and believe, but she felt scared, because for her, moving to Australia was a big move. She didn't know how she was going to do it. When I coached her to ask the universe for a sign, I added, 'What's the first thing that comes to mind?' Instantly, she said, 'A green convertible. Or no – a green Volkswagen convertible.' At the time I thought it was a pretty tall order for the universe, but it was summertime, so maybe it wasn't so tall. Then again, green wasn't such a popular color for a convertible. I asked her for an end time. She replied, 'Okay – by noon on Saturday.'

"Off she went. I got a text or an email from her a day later, and she said, 'You know, I was walking down Kensington and I think

I saw a green convertible Volkswagen driving down the street, but it was going so fast, I couldn't actually tell whether it was a Volkswagen or not.' She said, 'I don't think that counts.' I just said coyly, 'Okay, if that's what you want to believe!'

"A little while later—probably the next day or maybe even later that afternoon—I got another message from her. This one read, 'I'm at the dentist's office and I'm flipping through a magazine. There's a green convertible Volkswagen in the magazine. That doesn't count, right?' I answered, 'Do you want it to?' She figured that because it was in a magazine, it wasn't real, so that wasn't the real sign. Speed up to another day later, and she was walking out of her building where she worked. Right in front of the entry to the building—as in, she had to walk right past it—was a green convertible Volkswagen. This message read, 'Oh, no! I have to move to Australia, don't I?' There had been two pretty distinct signs that she really wanted to ignore, but she couldn't deny the third and very obvious one. The Universe had conspired and shown her where she needed to go, and now it was up to her to follow through and take action in that direction. Still she wasn't sure how it was all going to unfold, or how it was all going to work."

"Whoa, that's crazy! So did she go?" Pamela asked.

"We kept in touch for a little bit of time after that before I lost track of her for three or four years. I next saw her at a coaching event. She came up to me and very excitedly said, 'I just moved back from Australia. Let me tell you all about it!' I squealed, and stood in amazement as she shared her story about how it all unfolded magically and serendipitously once she said 'yes.' I got to hear about how the universe actually contrived to make it work for her, and how she landed a job right away and fell in love. I listened, in awe of all of the miraculous things that happened because she said 'yes' to the green Volkswagen convertible."

"Come on, you're telling me she also picked up and moved to Australia just because she randomly saw a car? What a fluke!"

"I'm not kidding! And I've got plenty more stories to match. Purple elephants, red balloons, red tulips…you name it. All of these clients were on the verge of a major life decision, and they knew they could either shrink back to their old life or expand into their new one. They asked the universe for a sign, and the universe brought it to them, or didn't. Because not seeing a sign is also a sign."

Pamela snorted, "A purple elephant? Seriously?"

Cathy laughed, "Seriously! That was a client who kept feeling the nudge to move to Tampa. So she thought she would one-up the universe by asking for a purple elephant. Still, a purple elephant turned up three times in the timeframe she had given! She once saw one on a belt buckle; once it was a ceramic piece she passed in a shopping mall—being viewed by a man wearing a Tampa Bay Lightning t-shirt, I might add!—and once on her favorite show that she had recorded during that designated time frame."

Pamela was still skeptical. "Well, I'm still not convinced."

Cathy laughed again, "Okay, one more then. I had another client – a performer living in New York. Her time there was due to end; however, she didn't want it to. So I asked her, 'What if you stay in New York?' She could not even comprehend the possibility of that, so again I suggested she ask for a sign. So she did. She asked to see a red balloon, if I'm not mistaken, by the next day at noon. She woke up the next day, and saw a red pig on the side of a building, not a red balloon. Then on her way to the studio she saw lots of differently colored balloons. Each time she was secretly relieved she hadn't seen a red balloon. Finally, sure enough, before her deadline, she saw another bunch of multi-colored balloons displayed by a street food vendor. Just as the wind parted the balloons, there, in their midst, was a big, bright, red one. She knew she was staying in New York."

"And?" Pamela said, still slightly skeptical.

"And she stayed! In fact, she still lives there. In Brooklyn. Happily working in theatre there, with her husband and a new baby. I could sit here all day telling you stories, but I'd rather say, 'Try it and you'll see.' In fact, why don't we try it right now?"

"Try it now? With what?" Pamela asked. Then she added cynically, "If I have breast cancer, show me a green balloon by tomorrow morning?"

Cathy said, "No, of course not. But what about starting with something small. What about whether or not you should pursue those pottery lessons. What do you think?"

"Okay," Pamela shrugged. "Seems harmless."

"Great. So, you want to ask the universe whether or not you should take those pottery lessons. If you are supposed to take the lessons, what do you need to see?"

Pamela looked up and thought for a moment. She saw a bird in the sky. "A feather."

"Okay – any color feather?"

"Ah," Pamela said, also thinking she could outsmart the universe. "A blue feather."

"Great. By when?"

"By 5 pm tomorrow." Pamela said, thinking to herself, Ha, universe. I'll be at the hospital all day tomorrow. No chance of a feather in there. Tomorrow she would be having her biopsy.

"Great. I'll call you at 5:01 tomorrow, to see if you found one," Cathy smiled. "After all, when you think about it, and look around, every day of our lives we're being shown signs. We have signs in our lives that we ignore and that we miss, or that we pretend aren't there – but they're there. Whatever shows up in our life, whether it's an argument with someone or a dirty look, or a feeling in our gut – whatever we see or don't see is always perfect because our life is trying to give us messages.

"Life is trying to give us clues as to what's next and, more often than not, it's in the form of feelings about something or someone. Those are our biggest clues: How we feel about someone's energy, or how we feel about doing something, or going somewhere. What we do is overlook them or run away from them. We pretend they're not there, but we can't unsee them once we've seen them! It can be something as simple as a glance or a dirty look, or a niggling in your gut, or a headache, or just that something doesn't feel right, and it's the feather or the whisper; the early warning signs that are trying to get your attention. You can listen to them and you can take some action, or you can ignore them and run away from them. You choose – but the signs will keep getting louder and bigger. You can run but you can't hide. You can never get away from them because they're there for you, not against you.

"I have a funny story about intuition. A number of years ago, I was shopping for my daughter's birthday present. I was in a mall, on my way out, when I remembered a CD that my daughter mentioned she wanted. It was a Tracy Chapman CD. She loved the song 'Fast Car.' I had gotten everything I needed, and I was pressed for time, yet I half-heartedly went back into the mall to get the CD. I went to the first music store and asked the clerk if they had it. They didn't.

I checked the only other store and they didn't have it either. I even called my son from the mall and asked if he had time to pick one up, but unfortunately he didn't. All of a sudden it became like a matter of life and death – I had to get this CD. Disappointed, I was leaving the mall, and a cute little dress in the window of a shop caught my eye. Although I didn't have time, I went inside. Wandering around, I asked myself, Why am I in here? Playing on the sound system was Tracy Chapman. Then I knew! I went up to the counter to see if the music was piped in from the mall, or if it was their music. The clerk looked at me strangely and said it was theirs. I couldn't believe my luck! I asked if the CD had the track I wanted on it. It did. So I asked if I could buy the CD from them. The manager said, 'Yes, you can have it!'

"I was overjoyed and giggly. It didn't have a case. I didn't care. I had the CD that I wanted, and I'd found it in a place I never would have guessed. Had I not trusted my gut and walked into that little dress shop I wouldn't have ever known what I would have missed! The clerk walked me down to the closest music store and got me a CD case. The next day I went back to that store and gave the manager $20 for her CD. I was so grateful."

Pamela shook her head again, "That's a crazy story. Okay, I'll give you the signs stuff, but I'm definitely not convinced that life happens for us. How could having a lump be good for me?"

Cathy interjected, "We don't know the answer to that yet, but I do know that this lump may just be an opportunity to look at your life differently, or it's the beginning of something even more amazing than you could imagine. What do we have if we don't believe or have faith that everything is here for our good, regardless of how it looks in this moment? This may be one of the greatest gifts you'll receive." Cathy sighed.

Pamela chuckled, "Right now it doesn't feel like I can believe in the universe, or signs. I'm just so worried. And everything you are saying is so…new. How have I never heard this before?"

Cathy answered, "It's not anything we learn in school, or from our parents or hear at the office. There are many people who share this concept, and it's becoming more mainstream and common knowledge, however it still has a long way to go for everyone to think this way. And honestly many people fear this way of thinking and living. Leaving something up to happenstance or trusting the power of the universe just sounds ridiculous to most. If you're willing, I'd like to share a little bit more about what I believe and what I know to be true for me."

"Oh, I'm willing, Cathy. I want to hear this!" Pamela lay down once again, this time beneath the tree on the summit, taking in the view of the mountains.

Cathy chose to sit the other way, and enjoyed the view of the valley. The sun hung high overhead, and Ellie stretched out at Cathy's feet, ready for another little nap as Cathy continued.

# Chapter 10

# The Gifts of our Emotions

"More often than not, difficult things are what wake us up. In my own life, my greatest awakening or awareness has always been found in my most challenging moments or adversity. It's found in my dark moments. Although it can be found in moments of happiness or joy, it is rare.

"Moments of raw awakening are found in those times when something is really challenging me in my life, or my body isn't feeling well. Those are the moments when I really need to turn and face myself and see what's going on for me because my body and life situations will always give me clues. If I don't do this right away, I remind myself it's like having a teacher that I don't listen to, that I'm ignoring or disregarding. It's like I've paid for this teacher and this course, yet I don't want to take on the knowledge."

"Um, you're saying I've asked for all this stress, this diagnosis and this unhappiness?" Pamela wasn't sure she liked the sound of that.

"On some level, yes. Life has a way of waking us up. Everything in our lives including our challenges, the obstacles on our path and everything that we see as things that we want to maneuver around or hop over or run away from, are gifts. Everything is a gift and a message in order for us to move forward.

"If you don't allow your lows, and if you don't find the richness in those lows, you miss matching those lows with incredible highs and joys because everything in life has an ebb and a flow. Ever heard of the saying, 'This too shall pass?'" Pamela nodded. "The dark moment is going to pass. Just as the joyous one will. Ebb and flow. But, if you don't have those really rich, dark moments where you dip in and you learn, you're not going to fully embrace the upswing of the happy moments and the joyous moments. Sometimes we think of the highs as positive things and the lows as negative things. However it's all part of the richness of our lives; the dark moments can be just as rich and delicious as the highs and the joy, if we allow them to be. When we allow ourselves to sit in that place of darkness, that may be where our greatest transformation is. That's the chrysalis.

"We live in a world where we don't honor our highs and lows, yet they are very much the same as the squiggly lines you see on a heart monitor. Those lines on the monitor indicate we're alive, and that we're emotional beings, having a full-on human experience. We're meant to feel everything – everything from the joy to the sadness. Somehow we're afraid of the sadness. When we prevent ourselves from feeling the negative emotion, whatever that is – the sadness or the anger or the disappointment, we prevent ourselves from also experiencing the highs – the rich happiness, joy and bliss, because by avoiding the negative, we also close off the positive. There must be balance. The contrast gives meaning to both. If you don't allow yourself to feel—really feel—the gritty, negative feelings, then there's no real joy in the moments of bliss because there's nothing to compare it to. Without night there is no day, without dark no light and so on. This provides us with contrast.

"Most of our discomfort comes about because we're neither happy nor sad. We find ways to numb out or pretend that we don't have to feel anything on either level. If you don't allow yourself to feel the lows, you won't experience the highs of the joy fully either. Everything will pass. Nothing stays forever. The joys don't stay forever because suddenly there's another challenge. The lows don't stay either – they come and go. It's like a teeter-totter. If you allow yourself to have this teeter-totter effect in your life, you get to experience the full range of emotion that comes with being human. Allowing yourself to feel your emotions and being present from moment to moment gives you the richness of life. You cannot control your emotions by trying to control what happens in your life. Let your emotions guide you and take you to the next experience or the next adventure or the next person you're supposed to meet or the next action that you're supposed to take in your life. When we stifle our emotions, we stop that process."

"Um, Cathy, it's a little hard to be taken seriously as a CFO if I'm constantly breaking down in tears. I mean, it was really hard getting out of there today without falling apart. I can't let my staff see me like that. Or my kids, for that matter. And I can't go around yelling at people, either."

"Sure, maybe you can't express your feelings in all places at all times, however you've got to let yourself feel them. Allow them to flow through you. Anxiety and depression come from not allowing the flow. We've got this dam built up that doesn't allow the water or the emotions to flow. That's what's so uncomfortable. That's where we feel like we have it all figured out even though we haven't got anything figured out. That's what prevents us from connecting with our true sense of self and our joy and our laughter and our love and our expansiveness and our sense of adventure and experience. We have no idea what's meant for us. We could never even imagine what's next for us because we have such a limited view of our own lives.

"It's like a picture of an iceberg: You can only see a part of it, but the big vast part is the part that's underneath the water that no one ever sees. That's what the universe can give you; the part that you can't even see. You just have to let go. You need to let go of the branch of safety and control because really, you don't have control. That two-by-four is going to come and get you. Possibly illness, divorce; whatever it is, it's going to get your attention. Get it at the whisper. Get it at the feather. Keep going downstream, allowing life to flow all around you. Embrace it and go. Say 'I'm curious about what's going to happen today. Take me on a ride universe, and let's go. Who am I going to meet today? What experience am I going to have today? Where are we going to go?' Get on that boat, and stop fighting the current."

Pamela rolled over onto her side. "Cathy, you make it all sound so easy. But I think I am afraid; I'm afraid every day. I don't know these things. I don't know about intuition. I just want to be happy. I don't want to change. How can you be so optimistic? What really makes you happy?"

Cathy turned to face Pamela, and saw the view of the Rockies rise up behind her. "It hasn't always been easy. My happiness is one of many emotions that has many different levels. Regardless of what happens in my life the undercurrent of my emotions is peace and joy. I allow myself to feel a full-range of emotions, as they rise and fall in any given moment. I am keenly aware that 'this too shall pass.' My goal isn't to be happy all the time, it's to welcome the gifts life shares with me – all of them. But I know it's a work in progress. I want to get the messages at a whisper. It's human nature to want to ignore it. Is that what you're doing right now?"

Pamela groaned, "Yes, that's entirely possible. Your thoughts are now really resonating with me."

"I'm so glad Pamela. You know, if you're willing to stand at that place where you know you have to go and walk through your adversity, it's a powerful way to live. It's like going through the birthing canal, so to speak – squeezing through this little tiny portal to get to the other side. It's painful and it's messy."

"Birthing process? Um, what? Please don't hit me with a butterfly-in-the-cocoon metaphor, now!" Pamela said, half-laughing, half-serious.

Cathy laughed and went on. "The whole birthing process—transformation—is not comfortable, and it's certainly not pretty. But once you get out on the other side, and you take your first breath and you see the world on the other side, it's magnificent. It makes all of that pain so worthwhile because there's beauty and there's pleasure and there's joy and different people to play with – people who are more like-minded and who understand and get who you are.

"You get the full range of experience and emotions and joy and pleasure and beauty and sadness and anger and vulnerability and all of those other things. You get to be fully alive and fully awake and fully present in this moment because this is the only moment that you can take any action."

Cathy explained: "When the process happens you're in this place where it's nice and warm and cozy. You want to stay in there because although it doesn't necessarily feel like you need to stay in there, you know that at some point you have to go through this passage. It's tight. It's dark. There's no room to maneuver. There's nowhere else to go except out. So, when you make the journey out from your uncomfortably comfortable life where you pretend everything is okay and you go on this journey through the birth canal it can be excruciating and messy. You might want to scream and you probably do and you have to wither your way through it, and it just feels like you're never going to get to the other side. Whatever that looks like, it's just too damn painful. You want to stop. You want to go back. But, you can't. There's nowhere to go. You can't go back to your numb little world in your little womb and pretend that you're not going through this.

"You've been evicted and out you go. There's something that's squeezing you—this thing called life—and you are being catapulted to the other side. You come out like a shot. It's like, 'Hello, world! Here I am! What the heck am I going to do now?' You look around and you go, 'Nothing looks familiar. Where am I? Am I all alone out here? Is there anybody out there?' When you come into this new world, you start to realize that there's hot. There's cold. There's light. There's bright. There's all kind of emotions. What is really there is freedom. You have choice. You no longer have to stay in a world where everything is controlled for you, and you have to feel like you have to be part of something. There is this sense of newness that comes into your life that allows you to feel new, free, alive and reborn, and you get giggly because it's like this is you for the first time. The butterfly is a really a good metaphor too! It's like seeing spring for the first time or seeing a bud on a tree or seeing a fish in the ocean or seeing color. You all of the sudden see what you haven't seen before. That can be exciting and scary at the same time, and you don't know what to do with it. But it's magnificent. It will feel like your whole life has been squeezed and wrung-out.

"When you emerge into the other side, you feel like there is nothing you can't do. Everything is within your reach; within your power. You start to make your own choices and decisions in your life, not based on what society or anyone else told you. You get to choose. You get to make a decision and take action in this moment. This is your life – no one else's. No one can tell you what to do or what you can't do. You're under your own steam, and you role model this for other people – possibly your children, and everyone else around you. You get to live your life your way, under no one else's rules. You're a bright light that will draw people to you. They want to emulate you. People will be in awe of what you can do and what you have done because of your courage to go through this process. If you're willing, my friend, you will be catapulted to the other side, and that will be magnificent."

"Sure, I hear you – but how do I do all of this and still stay at my job? And what happens to my family? I don't think I see how it can all connect. Surely something's gotta give?" Pamela asked.

"You have to let go of your illusion of control – the illusion of the dream, whatever that looks like. For me, my dream was this perfect relationship. I had this dream-like relationship – it was like a fairy-tale. Yet, my fairytale did not match the reality. I had to be willing to let go of my dream and let go of my whole world—at least the world how I thought it should look—in order to align with my true self and with where the universe was moving me toward. At this point, I don't know what that looks like, yet. And honestly that's the difficult part because I still feel vulnerable with the uncertainty.

"When you see your world starting to crumble, you may be in denial – in a deep state of unwillingness to face it and to change. Yet something altogether different will come out of the mess. It may be gritty and raw, and it is likely very uncomfortable. It quite often gets worse before it gets better; however, facing it head-on will always lead you to something better and more delicious. We must take a leap of faith, trusting that everything will turn out and often the results are beyond anything we could have imagined for ourselves."

Pamela put her hands on her face. "I just don't know if I can face this. Control and certainty is all I've ever known!" She moaned.

"Here's something to consider: What if what's happening to you and the uncertainty of this challenge takes you somewhere completely different than what you've envisioned for your life? And what if you know you're in the perfect place at the perfect time for what you're facing? That who you are is exactly who you are meant to be right now? There's no fixing. You are already as perfect right now as you will ever be. All you are is all you need to be at this moment. It doesn't mean that you won't learn and grow, and make changes when you're ready, but right here and now is all you need to be – full stop."

Pamela just shook her head again. She was beginning to understand, but still had doubts. "There is some comfort in hearing that, but I still have my doubts."

Cathy was empathetic. "You're not alone. And I know you're strong. I know you can make the changes when it feels right. And you may just start by making one small change – one simple change that you can make right now."

Pamela rolled back onto her back. "I can quit my job," she said, slowly and very, very quietly.

Cathy asked, "What was that? I didn't hear you."

Pamela repeated, even more quietly, "I could quit my job."

"Mmmhmmm. Wow. And how does that feel?"

Pamela looked at Cathy. "Scary and exciting!"

Cathy smiled. "Then I think it's a great idea!"

# Chapter 11

# Your Experience Is Up To You

The sun had shifted and began its western descent before the women decided to make their way back down the trail. Cathy took the hike down as an opportunity to boost Pamela's courage.

"One of the most important steps," Cathy began, "is to come into alignment with yourself and make an agreement with yourself in your life that you're turning inward and not turning outward; that you're putting yourself first, by honoring your values and what matters most to you, and by setting boundaries. By saying no to others, you're really honoring yourself – you're really saying yes to you."

"I truly can't imagine what that would be like. Saying yes to me? Feels really selfish, actually." Pamela said, stepping lightly down the trail as they wound their way downhill.

"Selfish? Hardly! Selfish gets such a bad rap. Here's something to consider: What about being…Self-Full? When you say yes to you, you unleash an enormous amount of energy and clarity which results in greater capacity for love and passion and purpose. You become the author and creator of your own life. You see your own inner wisdom shining through. You get to the core of who you are, and that shines. That light emanates from within you.

"As you start to shine, and become self-full, you begin attracting more of the things that give you who you are to mirror yourself back to you. Everything you need in your life starts to appear. Things begin to unfold for you in mysterious and magical ways and in positive ways. You notice that something that may not have worked before suddenly works in your favor, or it takes you in a different, more exciting direction. And if it doesn't, you can tweak it. You can start to adjust what doesn't feel right because you have an inner compass – that knowing and that belief in yourself, that if you are out of alignment with you, you can feel it.

"As you become more aware and awake in your life, you start to realize that you can no longer lie to yourself. You can lie to yourself for a short time, or trick yourself into believing something, but it catches up with you. It catches up with you quicker. When you didn't have this knowledge or this sense of self, you were able to get away with it. Now, you become higher up on the food chain, and the stakes become higher. You begin to realize that you can no longer get away with what you used to get away with. There's no more pretending. The universe has a way of giving you notes and giving you nudges and giving you clues much quicker and louder and stronger for you to get back into alignment. It's really for your good, which is keeping you on your course.

"Your inner guidance system gets you back on course quicker once you know something doesn't feel right. You know when you're slipping out of integrity, and you simply get back on course. You make small adjustments here and there, like a sailboat correcting its course when the wind changes, or suddenly stops. You navigate around life: What you bump up against, people who's energy doesn't feel right. It's course correction; a tweak here, a tweak there. You don't fight the current, you go with the flow of life. You get back on the boat, and you get back into the flow. It's like bumper cars. If you bump up against another car, you know to move away from it.

"It becomes a dance down the river. As Abraham-Hicks reminds us, 'You don't have to struggle and fight to get your desires. Let go of the oars...everything you want is downstream,' meaning, stop paddling upstream – everything that you need and desire is yours when you simply allow yourself to go with the flow of life. You will be taken care of, and that which you believe you deserve will come your way. That is the optimum phrase: Believe you deserve. More often than not we don't believe we deserve abundance, prosperity, happiness and joy in our lives, which prevents it from actually flowing toward us. That which we receive, or don't receive, also mirrors our belief about what and how much we deserve. If we have a scarcity mentality, the universe matches it exactly. Once you change how you feel about yourself, and what you believe you deserve in this life, the universe will deliver to match your desires. When you change within, you see it in the physical, externally.

"I had a teacher and mentor tell me once that if you don't go within, you go without. Anything that you believe you deserve will start to come towards you because it will again prove you right. We say things like, 'See? I didn't get that promotion,' or, 'I knew that relationship wouldn't work out.' How often do we prove ourselves right by declaring that something we want cannot possibly happen? Through all of this, you really have to come face to face with your own uncertainty, with not being able to control everything. Believe it or not, you can actually control your future – by letting go of the oars and going downstream. It's easier said than done, and completely terrifying for many, many people. Feeling like we're in control gives us a sense of safety, like we've got all of our ducks in a row. It's really a false sense of safety, but safety nonetheless."

"I don't believe it. How can I possibly…?" Pamela trailed off.

Cathy explained. "Your belief about yourself and your intuition is what controls the future. For example, if you believe that something is going to be difficult, guess what? Most likely it will be difficult. If you believe that something will go smoothly, you're probably right. There we go proving ourselves right again! There will be moments in your life that feel uncomfortable. What you perceive them to mean and how you navigate them will be your greatest next step. Life can be wonderful or it can be terrible, or it can be mediocre. You choose!"

"So can I choose to get a positive result from the biopsy tomorrow?" Pamela asked.

"It's more about choosing how you want to face the result, whatever it is. Whatever you choose is perfect because whatever shows up for you will be exactly as you imagined. It may look different, but it will be wonderful or it will be terrible. It's up to you. What is the experience you want?

"We have been conditioned to expect everything, such as this lump, to be difficult and hard. What if it's your greatest gift? Your second chance to live your life exactly how you want? Your opportunity to really look to see if what you're doing in life aligns with who you truly are? Or what if it was created for you, by you, out of fear and wanting to feel safe? Fear is made up. It's a feeling based on past events that keep us reliving something that may have scared us in the past, or we heard it on the news that we should be scared, or we collectively as a society have deemed something should be feared. If you take each moment as a fresh new experience, without the baggage of the past biasing your decision, you will have a different experience than the last one – if you keep an open mind and don't let fear run the show, that is.

"I once had a client who was doing her PhD, and she kept telling me how hard it was. She was really stressed, and it was taking her a very long time to complete it, to the point that she wanted to quit. So one day I asked her, 'Where did you get the idea that doing your PhD was so hard?' and she said, 'Everybody I know who's ever done a PhD has said it's hard work.' I said, 'Is it hard work?' She said, 'Not really – it's been really interesting and kind of fun.' So I asked, 'Then why do you tell yourself that it's hard work?' She stopped and she re-alized that she had just bought into the whole belief that it's difficult because that's what she had been told. Not only that, she had been causing herself stress because of this.

"We think that if something's worth having, it's hard – that it's going to be difficult and going to be a hard path to go down. But that's not always true. Even with your diagnosis right now, what are your first thoughts about it?"

"That the lump is cancerous. That I'll have to do chemo. That I'll lose my hair and be really sick for a long time. Maybe even…" Pamela stopped herself.

Cathy jumped in. "And is it possible that the lump is not cancer-ous? Are you aware of the nature of our breasts and the lumps that can form with or without cancer cells connected? Or, is it possible the lump is cancerous but you're getting it so early that you easefully manage treatment?"

Pamela shook her head.

"Did you know there are alternatives? Have you considered there may be alternative ways of thinking and perceiving the entire situation?"

Pamela shook her head again, "Well no…not really."

"Okay. If you're willing, let's explore this, shall we?"

Pamela nodded.

"What I'm suggesting is that you can actually change how you feel about the outcome of the diagnosis by how you think about it. Look at this as an opportunity to make new choices in your life rather than looking at it as a struggle or a death sentence. And the same goes for any difficulty in your life.

"Sure, there may be some struggles. There may be some challenges along the way. But really, if you look at the overall picture, how do you want YOUR experience to be? How do you want to show up? How do you want to show up within that context? Do you want to have a positive experience? Whether something is difficult or whether it is easy – that's not the point. The point is, what experience do you want to get out of it? If you want to get a terrible experience out of it, good. Perfect. That's what you shall have. That will be a great story, because we love to tell the stories about how difficult things are."

The women laughed at this.

"I don't know about that…although I guess I do tend to get on the complain train a lot, especially with some of my colleagues." Pamela confessed.

"Right? And have you noticed that we don't always get an audience when things are going great and when things are going really smoothly? That's not where we get the attention. A lot of times, we get the attention when something's really difficult, whether it actually is, or not. Whatever you bump up against and whatever obstacle or challenge is in your way, it will have to be dealt with. You can deal with it with humor and joy, or with disdain and bitterness. The experience you have is totally up to you. Everything in your life has to be dealt with. Whether you do it now with a whisper or a feather or you choose wait to until the proverbial big truck hits you. You will have to deal with it. To go through these struggles and these challenges is what it's like to be human. The human experience can be positive and beautiful and humbling and extraordinary!"

Cathy paused for effect before continuing. "Once you make a decision and once you take action, there will be a ripple effect in your life. It's like painting a wall in your home or changing the color of your furniture or changing the carpet. Once you change one thing, you realize how all of the other rooms need to be repainted and how the carpet in the other rooms need to be switched out; or if you buy a new appliance and it's a different color, then you need to buy all new stainless steel appliances. That's the ripple effect of making a change in your life. It can sometimes prevent people from doing things, because they know that one change, big or small, may change many things, or everything."

"Yeah, and that's definitely something that worries me. One change will impact lots of things – including my kids, my husband, our financial situation…" Pamela said.

"Your health…" Cathy added.

Pamela nodded.

"Here's the beautiful part, though: Everything in your life does change. It changes for the better. It changes in far more magnificent ways than you could ever imagine. Saying 'no' to being a victim of your circumstances can change everything in your life. It can change how you see your life. It can change how people see you. Sometimes that can be really scary for people. Once you start doing this work and once you start honoring yourself and seeing how it feels for you, it will motivate and inspire you to want more for your life and to take action. It becomes a matter of never wanting to go back to feeling numb and uncomfortably comfortable. For me, this way of life feels so much better, even though I still have many unknowns in front of me now.

"Being in a place of unhappiness, misery and not sleeping—all of those things that become the norm, the new status quo and who we describe ourselves to be—that's not who we are. That's not who we're meant to be. We're meant to be joyous, healthy, loving, open creatures. What prevented us from being just that? Life – someone else's version of life, but not ours. Starting today, we can change that!"

They arrived back down to the bottom of the trail, and began hiking along the flat.

Cathy continued. "We can't see all the things going on behind the scenes, and if we could, then we may be a lot more patient. I believe there's a matrix or an overall plan for our lives, and we have opportunities to choose, of course, but no matter what, this plan will always find us, and it will always find us at the times that are right and that we're ready for, because sometimes we're just not ready, or the other people involved aren't ready, or that opportunity still needs to take shape. Who knows what's in store for us? I say to clients, 'If you could see your whole life laid out in front of you, like a roadmap, you would see the enormous potential, and just how big and magnificent it looks. It's so big that you probably wouldn't even take a step forward! It would scare the crap out of you!' But by just taking one step at a time, we get there. Like climbing a mountain – one step at a time."

Pamela and Cathy shared a laugh at the thought. "Like this hike today!"

"Exactly. That's why we aren't given the whole outline. It's too massive and amazing. We would be so intimidated that we'd just probably just stay in bed all day! Think of it – if Oprah knew when she was 8 years old who she was going to become she too might have thought, "Oh, that's just too big for me!" That's why we take it a step at a time and a day at a time.

"It was the same with that pull to move to Australia, too. I didn't know why I went. I didn't even know I ever wanted to go. It was my first ever coaching client and her energy – that was the pull. I now believe that had been pulling me all along. I was meant to go to Australia to help her do what she needed to do. That thought would never leave me; I could never get it out of my mind. It also happened with one of my relationships too."

Pamela was walking behind Cathy. "Oh? How so?"

"Well, I actually met a boy when I was 11, and I knew I loved him right in that moment. We would see each other from time to time in our small town – we spoke but never dated. I just admired him from afar. I never saw him again after he turned 16. I never knew where he went or why he left. After my relationship with my kids' Dad ended, thoughts of that boy I met 32 years earlier were beginning to come back and haunt me. Back then, I didn't know about intuition or the universe conspiring for my highest good. I just kept fighting thoughts of him. Several months went by, and then one night I dreamt I met him. I knew that was the sign that I needed to contact him. Even then, without knowing what I know now I'm certain it was getting me ready for a new relationship with him. The time had finally become right. It haunted me so much that I needed to track him down! And I did."

"And then?" Pamela wanted to know.

"Ah, Pam." Cathy smiled. "That's a story for another hike." They laughed.

Cathy quickly redirected the conversation. "It's a process. When you're ready to hear the next lesson, or place that one piece into the grand puzzle, you take action and do it. But you can't force it. You're not ready until you or the universe is ready. You may not think you're ready but it's going to make you ready."

"Well, I can definitely say I'm not ready!" Pamela said.

Cathy laughed. "No one ever is!"

"But I'm willing to try that 'ask the universe' thing."

"Oh? Really?" Cathy said, surprised.

"Yeah. This time to ask about quitting my job. This whole time we've been walking it's been haunting me, as you say, to ask the question. So if I'm supposed to quit my job, I need to see a blue feather by tomorrow at 5 pm." Pamela stated with conviction.

"Wow, Pam!" Cathy said. "Let's see, shall we?"

Cathy grinned at Pam as they approached another hill on the trail.

# Chapter 12

# Keep Climbing

As they approached the hill, which was the biggest ridge to crest so far, Pamela groaned. "We just climbed a hill! Ah! When are we going to be done?"

Cathy laughed, "Come on. We can do it." She chuckled as she remembered something, and said, "Speaking of which, clients would ask me all the time, 'When am I going to be done? When am I going to have this all figured out?' I'm here to tell you, you're never going to be done. There's always going to be another hill to climb, another mountain to appreciate, another valley to explore… Somebody should really tell us that when we start this journey!"

Cathy giggled before continuing. "We think we're here for a good time, to work and make money, to buy bigger houses and fancier cars…and yes, all of that is quite delicious; however, we're really here to learn and grow and awaken and become aware of who we truly are. We are here to grow as spiritual beings – to help one another become our best selves, and celebrate our peaks, and help each other through our valleys. As we learn one lesson, we move on to the next one. It's just like climbing a mountain – or hiking the trail we're on today! We must always keep moving forward."

Pamela muttered, "Evidently."

Cathy said enthusiastically, "You start at the base, and depending on your challenge or your obstacle on the mountain, you either do some hard climbing, or it's an easy hike or a walk. You get to the top and you go, 'Ahh, I'm here. This is great. I can see the world from all vantage points – what a beautiful view. I must have figured it out now that I'm done climbing.' The view up there is very nice for a period of time, long or short. Then as you're going along you see there's another mountain to climb. You once again start at the bottom and you climb your way up the top of that hill or mountain, with the challenge, the obstacles, and those magnificent lessons. You slug your way to the top, and you get to the top of the mountain. You go, 'Ahh! I'm here. I've figured it out.' You stand up there, looking out from the top of the mountain feeling quite smug and proud of yourself. Then as you're watching the view and enjoying it, you see there's another mountain or a hill. It might not be a mountain. It might just be a knoll this time. There's always something around the corner. There's always another challenge or AFGO."

"Right – like your friend says, another frickin' growth opportunity."

"Yes! Life is our school. We don't have to sign up for any other course. Life gives us that. Life gives us the opportunity to learn and grow. Life 101, 201, a million and four. We get to learn every single day – we just have to be open and willing. What do we have to lose?"

"Nothing I guess…when you put it that way," Pamela said.

"If you want, you can remain here, stuck. I'm not going to make assumptions. We can all stay in places that don't challenge us to grow – those familiar places that help us feel safe yet uncomfortably comfortable. Some even make us feel like we're wearing a straight-jacket, whether it's a job you despise, or a relationship that no longer works, or is physically or emotionally abusive, or a friendship that you feel you have an obligation to that you've simply outgrown. Have you heard the saying that familiarity breeds contempt? It's about putting up with things that no longer work for us. If that's what you want, that's okay. I'm not going to judge you or your decisions. Every moment of every day, you get to choose.

"When you climb that mountain, that adversity or challenge, and you get to the top, you overcome that obstacle and you look down over the vast expanse, well, it feels amazing. The view up there is spectacular, because you did it.

"Why not live this way? What holds us back? Why do we feel it's too uncomfortable or too dangerous? What prevents us? Kids are learning all the time. They adjust, maneuver around obstacles and other kids on the playground and food they don't like. At one point as we grow up do we learn to tolerate it? We numb ourselves out in order to prevent ourselves from really being honest with ourselves about what we want and what we don't want – what feels good and what doesn't."

"I guess we do," Pamela said. She paused to catch her breath, watching Cathy keep going up the next steep passage, Ellie close on her heels.

# Chapter 13

# ...And it Happens Again

"By the way," Cathy said, as they crested the ridge and began once more on the flat path towards the trailhead. "It's not like we have one big moment of crisis and decision in our lives, where we blow our lives up and move on. I thought my huge change in my 40's was significant, and here I am, now in my 50's, and still reeling from even more shake-ups. I don't want to scare you, but what's happening right now is what's happening right now for you, and then it will be over and you will be fine, and then it will be onto the next one. This is life. This is expansion."

Pamela walked alongside Cathy, "Oh, dear. I hope you're not right! I don't think I can handle so much shaking up."

"Well," Cathy retracted her words slightly, "everyone is different; we all receive the messages differently and we are all on different points along the path, so of course your experience will be uniquely yours. For me, I just want to catch the messages at the feather. I'm ready to expand and trust my intuition. No more trucks, please!

"I really see now how my last relationship was such a profound gift. I see how indifferent I had become in my marriage. The first time I came across a passage in Brené Brown's The Daring Way about indifference and betrayal I nearly crawled out of my skin. I hadn't been able to put my finger on what was happening in my relationship, but it was indifference. It's such a cold, disconnected word. By definition, indifference means 'lack of interest, concern or sympathy.' In other words, feeling something is insignificant, unimportant or irrelevant and having a lack of interest…you get the picture. That was me to myself, showing up in my relationship mirrored back to me."

"Cathy, I had no idea. You felt that way the whole time?" Pamela asked gently.

"Not necessarily, but how it was showing up in my daily life was as a genuine lack of interest in the events in my life – where I went, who I saw, what I did and what I liked."

"So hang on, where's the gift? I don't get it." Pamela said.

"The gift?" Cathy repeated. "Well, I realized my partner was simply mirroring my behavior. I was the one who was indifferent toward myself! By that I mean, I was running as far as I could from myself. I was indifferent to what I wanted in my life, my desires, dreams and my values. I made my life become unimportant and irrelevant and I lacked interest in everywhere I went, who I saw, what I did and what I liked. I completely lost myself. And he was simply my mirror.

"I had a lot going on in my early 50's. I became an empty-nester. My two children were gone, and although I was happy to see them independent I grieved their departure from the home. It left a huge hole in my life. If I wasn't needed as a Mom, who was I? It was huge, and totally unexpected. Thankfully, I found some validation in what I was feeling when I read The Wisdom of Menopause. Christiane Northrup first introduced me to the concept of the empty-nest syndrome in her book."

"Something to look forward to, I guess?" Pamela said sarcastically.

Cathy laughed. "It happens to all of us my friend! And for me it was harder than I had expected! I didn't see myself as someone who would grieve being a full-time Mom. It showed up as feelings of loneliness, neediness, feeling sorry for myself, withdrawing, and self-criticism. I really questioned what kind of a parent I was, and felt guilty for what I had and hadn't done. Was I too hands-off? Were my kids too independent? I could have easily let them live at home until they were 25 or 30, or longer. Without them I felt so alone.

"In this dark place I realized I wanted someone to take care of me to buffer my becoming an empty-nester, and the onset of peri-menopause. They were both completely off my radar as challenges in my life, and threw me for a loop. I really thought I had this. When both engulfed me at around the same time, it was a double whammy of emotions and turmoil. My life, as I had known it, was completely changed. Why was my body doing this 'to me'?"

"Wait a second – 'to you?' But life happens for us, doesn't it?" Pamela questioned Cathy.

"Absolutely – however I had to experience this pain to remind myself. I told myself I didn't have time to feel the sting of any of it. I was too busy taking care of everyone else. A great diversion. A brilliant distraction from what I really needed to do, which was take very good care of me: Feel all my emotions, cry from my soul for what I felt I had lost; yet instead, I poured my energy into my work, taking care of my client's needs, all the while running as fast away from myself as possible.

"The pain of being on my own and my body shifting was one of the darkest places I have ever known. I wouldn't fully allow myself to go there. I only dipped a toe or two into that pool, then jumped back out again. I still felt so alone – and because of this, I was vulnerable.

"Because of my vulnerability, I left myself wide open for betrayal, which ended up being a theme and a gift of my last relationship. I may have unknowingly fallen into the relationship in order to soothe myself. It worked, for a while. I'm not sure if indifference is a form of betrayal; however, I do know it's damaging to the person on the receiving end."

"What do you mean by betrayal?"

"By definition, betrayal is a broken agreement – something considered vital to the intregrity of a relationship. It can be many things. Yet I wonder how often we betray ourselves without giving it a thought. We'll say 'yes' when we mean 'no.' We'd rather disappoint ourselves than disappoint others, throwing ourselves under the bus for the approval of others. Observing myself in the face of this betrayal that was happening externally, I ended up uncovering what was really going on inside emotionally. It was grief."

"Grief? But who died?" Pamela asked.

"Grief was such a powerful emotion for me, Pamela. Grief can be more than the death of a loved one; it can be the death of a relationship, the death of a career or the ending of something important to us. Death and loss happen all around us. I am only just now learning how much grief I was carrying around inside of me, and it just needed to be felt, processed and expressed. You probably have a lot, too, and you just don't know it yet.

"For me, I eluded grief for five decades. I did a really good job of outrunning it! I outsmarted it and even congratulated myself on not experiencing anything remotely close to it. Then it hit me. All of a sudden. And it wanted out."

"Let me guess: You got really sick?" Pamela said in earnest.

"Yep," Cathy said. "Profound fatigue and a lung infection. At first, it didn't seem serious. Then it became pneumonia. I had it before; I thought I knew what to expect. A few days on the couch and I would be well again. Not this time. I was flat-out on the couch for eight weeks."

"Eight weeks! That was some pneumonia. What was the difference between the last time you had it and this time?"

"I could no longer escape my feelings. I experienced a profound sense of grief that turned into depression…or was it the other way around? I wasn't a depressed person. I'm the 'glass half-full' person – optimistic and cheerful in the face of adversity. This was different. What was going on? I had succumbed to a profound sadness. During this time I was reminded of a quote I had read by Debbie Ford: 'You must go into the dark in order to bring forth your light.' It was really my dark night of the soul."

"The dark night of the soul? What do you mean?" Pamela asked.

"Well, it's like what I was saying before, that our greatest gifts are revealed in our darkest moments. This illness was a gift to help me see what I had been running from all those years – decades even. I had to face it all: Several failed relationships, the sudden death of family members, betrayal in friendships, the changing role as a mother with my kid's departure from the nest and the transition in my coaching career. So many things that I had pretended didn't affect me all of a sudden did, and in a profound and significant way. They were demanding to be seen and to be acknowledge, now.

"You cannot keep grief locked away inside. It may become depression over time, which will then begin to engulf your joy and eat away at your soul. I thought that if I allowed myself to feel either sadness or grief, that I would fall into a dark pit that would eventually swallow me up and that I wouldn't be able to get out. It's exactly the opposite. In order to find happiness and joy we must go into those dark places and feel the pain. The only way to get past it is to stick with it and go through it. Otherwise it comes around again, more painful, deeper and darker. I was at that place. I could no longer outrun it.

"We cannot live in perpetual bliss and happiness. It simply isn't sustainable for long periods of time. There must be ups and downs, like those zig-zagging lines on a heart monitor associated with a heart-beat. Those highs and lows emulate the rhythm of our life. Can you picture it? Without the pulse it becomes a straight line, and you know what that means?"

"Death?" Pamela mused.

"Yes, in a way! It becomes mediocre, monotone and flat. Without lows, there are no highs. When you carry around your pain, instead of facing it head on, grieving it and mourning it, it will come back to haunt you with a vengeance. It will keep trying to get your attention, by causing you more pain and suffering, all the while grinding you down, preventing you from a restful sleep and other things…until you give it the necessary attention it deserves and is demanding from you. Once and for all.

"I was so fortunate to have the time to go through this grief process. The universe completely cleared my schedule; I was on hiatus from my coaching career, my kids were gone, I had moved to a different city and I was alone a lot of the time. I had no other choice but to go through it. Most days I didn't actually know what I was grieving. It didn't make sense. I had to let go of figuring it out. Whatever feeling was inside of me, wanted out, and I didn't have to pick through the garbage to find it. I cried, I journaled and I wrote my morning pages – which I had learned from reading The Artist's Way, that book that was given to me so long ago now."

"Morning pages? What's that?" Pamela was curious.

"Morning pages are Julia Cameron's brilliant technique for the purging of our thoughts: Three full unlined pages of ranting and ramblings making no sense to anyone, and especially you. They're like a defragging of our daily thoughts, beliefs about ourselves and patterns that keep us stuck and going around in circles in our minds. It's not pretty, and it needs to go out with the rest of trash. They're not fit for human consumption, or review. It is a magical process and it always amazes me how powerful it is."

"So you write a bunch of crap that no one will ever read? What's the point of that?" Pamela asked. To Pamela, if she was going to write anything, it better serve a tangible purpose.

"Oh – it's the process of dumping unnecessary thoughts and beliefs. It's about the process of letting it all go and discarding those thoughts; unloading all your feelings and thoughts… Try it sometime."

"Okay, I'm willing to give it a try, only because you say it works," Pamela agreed.

"I've heard we have something like 60,000 thoughts in a day, and 2/3 or more of them are thoughts we had yesterday, last month, last year and a decade or more ago."

"Wow, really?" Pamela laughed. "No wonder I can't seem to relax."

Cathy laughed. "I'll tell you something else – you sure know who your friends are when they're willing to listen to you re-tell your story over and over and over again at nauseum. A dear friend and her husband drove to Calgary to rescue me since I wasn't healing and took me to their home on Vancouver Island. That was my healing place. It was a place of solace and refuge – no judgment or expectations. I lay on their couch for a week before I began to feel alive again."

"During that time another friend sent me a great quote from the author, Zayn Malik. I think it went something like this: 'Turning the page is the best feeling in the world because you realize there's so much more to the book than the page you were stuck on.' It's such a good quote, because it's so true! Something shifted the day I read that and I realized I had told my story long enough. I was even boring the crap out of myself, so I could only imagine what my friends thought. I declared right then and there I would no longer repeat it. The sun began to come out and my life turned around. I began to see life through a different lens. I had clarity and a new focus. I realized I started to wake up happy each morning, without an external reason. I didn't need some thing or some one to make me happy. I could be happy within – just me. That was the day I knew I was all I really needed."

"So, what was the lesson? Or should I say, the gift?" Pamela asked, listening intently.

"Out of that time came the inevitable: I needed to take care of me and separate from my relationship. It wasn't healthy for me, and I was sinking into a pit of despair and heartache. What I really needed was time alone to begin to heal my soul. I had willingly given myself away in order to make things okay for someone else. I had been willingly buffering and carrying the pain in my relationship, because that's what we do for loved ones, right? I was trying to save him. It was then that I realized I could only save myself.

"All my life I have seen the good in people and their amazing potential. As a coach, I see it all the time, and if they're willing to see it I can help them see it too. Not everyone wants to see it, or believe it. People can't always see it – often something else gets in the way; primarily their belief about themselves and their lack of self-worth and knowing that they are enough just as they are.

"I shared with a close friend, years before I became a coach, the vision I saw for her life. I didn't tell her what she wasn't; I simply told her what I thought she was capable of. From that day on, despite my attempts to make contact with her, we didn't see each other for several years. One day she invited me for lunch, and acknowledged that she, too, was finally able see her own potential, and that she was taking action in her life to aspire to her greatness. She said that during the time we were apart she could hear my words and they kept haunting her, but that she wasn't ready to embrace them until she let go of what wasn't working in her life. Today she never ceases to amaze me with what she has created and accomplished. She has gone far beyond what I could have ever imagined. She wasn't ready 'til she was ready, but now, look out!"

Cathy paused, and the women walked in silence for a few meters before Cathy shared again. "The most difficult part for me during my own time of darkness was trusting that there was something more magnificent on the other side; that the sun would come out after the rain. In my heart I knew it to be true, however when you're in the thick of it, it doesn't seem possible at times. And yet when it does happen, there's always a magnificent rainbow to celebrate all the effort it took to get there. The universe celebrates along-side us when we do our inner work.

"For me, the darkness was realizing how I had sold out on myself; not setting my boundaries, tending to someone else's well-being and pouring my energy somewhere it wasn't needed or wanted: into someone who didn't want it, and didn't ask me for it. I was well-meaning. But who did I think I was, thinking I knew more than him about what he needed for his life? I realized I didn't. We're all on a journey. Mine isn't any better than someone else's, and their journey isn't any less important if it doesn't match mine. Hard lesson. I now know what it means to say, 'The more I know the less I know.'" Cathy giggled. "It's up to each one of us to sow our own harvest, plant our own seeds and water and weed our own garden. We reap the beautiful bounty."

Pamela listened as she walked, taking in every word.

"Even harder has it been to watch my kids make mistakes—especially the ones similar to mine—and not want to help them or do it for them, just to ease their suffering. I've found experience is the best teacher. Without it we don't fully grow. We all have to learn from our own mistakes, when we're ready to make them, and not before. I can't prevent something from happening for someone. I can only role model a new behavior or overcome an obstacle of my own with dignity and grace, and trust they will do the same. We can, however, hold their hand, or their heart, while they're going through it."

They walked a little in silence. A breeze picked up and Cathy smiled in the face of it.

"You know, Pamela," Cathy began, "Looking back over the years, I really feel both a sense of regret and awe. I keep wondering whether I screwed up my life, or if it's the most amazing one. My heart feels one thing, and my head still wants to tell me another!" Cathy laughed.

"Oh, Cathy," Pamela said. "I think it's the most amazing life. I wish I could be so brave."

Cathy looked at Pamela and smiled. "I've had some amazing things happen in my life, it's true. With each failed relationship, I have learned more and more about myself and what I need to do to honor the authentic person that I am. I learned how I had tried to save the other person and that I really can't – I can only save myself. I can only learn about myself.

"I can't change anyone or make somebody be the way I want them to, and I can't morph or turn myself into a chameleon in order to be loved. At the root of my adversity was the feeling that I wasn't enough and wanting to be loved, and then being whoever that person wanted me to be in order to receive it."

"But don't we all do that? Isn't that what everyone wants?"

Cathy went on, "Yes, but what a waste of time it has been! I wish so much that I could turn the clock back. Oh, to be a decade or two younger, only to have the wisdom I have now."

Pamela chuckled. "And only moments ago, you told me that we don't get the lessons until we are meant to get the lessons. We don't move and grow until the time is ripe. The stars line up. Right?"

Cathy laughed. "You're right. When I think this way, I soon realize I only want to beat myself up instead of realizing it's all part of the plan. It's all part of the magnificence of why we're here. Sure, we're here to have fun, but I believe we're here to be spiritual growth-mongers. We're here to learn lessons and evolve our souls, and if we don't, then we wither and die. I look back at all the things I have in my life where I feel I've failed and really, they're not failures. They're life lessons. Life is for us. It's not against us. All the things that happen, these are gifts, magnificent gifts. As I reflect back on my life I realize that I was here to really love myself. I wasn't here to find happiness from external things, like a career, or a relationship, or skydiving, but to find it within. Now, regardless of whether I have all of those things or none, I can honestly say I wake up happy. Happy for no reason. At my core, I feel joyful within myself, and that's a powerful gift! It's something all of us are searching for.

"So much of my life has been a test. Am I going to get it with a whisper? A feather? Or does a bus have to fall on me? I want to get my lessons at a whisper. I want to get that knowing that something doesn't feel right the first time and not wait 5 or 10 years or until there's an illness or something so loud I can't ignore it.

"We all know when we begin to feel there's a crack in the foundation – something that doesn't feel right or smell right. I want to be the person who questions it right away. It doesn't mean you have to walk away, it just means making different and better choices for yourself. I now listen to what my gut is telling me without question. Maya Angelou so wisely said, 'When people show you who they are, believe them – the first time.' Meaning, when something doesn't feel right, believe it the first time. Don't wait and question it, don't try to make it okay and don't morph or turn yourself into something to fit in or to make it feel okay. It's there to give you an opportunity to make different and better choices for yourself, and to steer you in the right direction for your life. When we ignore the signs they get louder, stronger, and more and more messy. If we can align ourselves with the messages early on we save ourselves a lot of grief and years – even decades."

Pamela smiled, "I think this conversation might save me a lot of grief. I feel much better than I did before we started hiking, that's for sure."

Cathy was pleased. "Well, I'm optimistic for you. I know you are in it right now, and it doesn't feel like a gift, but believe me. This is a gift. This is your gift. You can open it when you're ready and do something amazing with it. And I can't wait to see where this leads you."

Pamela laughed, "Ha! Me too." She looked ahead and saw they were approaching the end of the trail. "I can't believe it – we did the whole hike!" She looked at her watch. "And if I hadn't left work today, I'd be in a meeting right now, post-lunch, wishing desperately that I could take a nap."

Cathy smiled at her friend. "And aren't you so glad you honored yourself and didn't stay?"

Pamela nodded wholeheartedly.

"What's your next step, then?" Cathy asked.

"That's a good question. Morning pages!" She laughed, "Of course, I have to get a reading list—Louise Hay is on it—and I really feel I'd like to learn to meditate. I think I may know someone who can help me." She winked at Cathy.

"I think so too!" Cathy said.

The women paused at the trailhead and looked back at the hill they had summited and the ridge they had walked along. Both women inhaled deeply, the pine-scented air filling their lungs. Pamela turned to Cathy with tears in her eyes.

"Thank you for sharing your story, Cathy." Pamela said. The women shared a warm, long embrace.

After they broke apart, Cathy said, "You know, I felt a lot of peace this morning when I awoke. I just want you to know, that it is available to you too. You will find it, my friend. Trust."

Pamela nodded and wiped her eyes, grinning. She looked around, then burst out laughing.

"What's so funny?" Cathy asked, following Pamela's gaze, but not seeing what was making her laugh so much.

"Don't you see it?" Pamela asked, pointing to the ground just ahead of them.

Cathy looked, and started to laugh.

There it was, laying near a rock, on top of a few spruce needles: A blue feather.

Cathy turned to Pamela, "Aren't you going to pick it up?"

Pamela hesitated, then picked it up. She laughed, tears in her eyes, as she marveled at the feather, blue, with black stripes, and a white tip. A blue jay feather.

She looked at Cathy, awestruck. "I guess I'm going to pottery class!" She laughed, then frowned a little. "After I quit my job, that is."

Cathy laughed, "Life is speaking to you. And you are listening! Let's go home and celebrate."

Pamela nodded, gazing at the feather.

The women shared a warm embrace. They linked arms and happily marched out of the forest, smiling, Ellie picking up the pace to follow.

# About the Author

Cathy Yost is an Internationally trained and accredited Personal Life Coach. Since 2004, after her own leap of faith called her to leave an unfulfilling career, start over and move her family to Australia for a year, Cathy has been inspiring people to trust their intuition and listen to the calling of their souls. Providing a space where only truth can reside, Cathy is a sounding board, adept at respectfully honoring each individual journey with patience and wisdom.

Cathy lives a simple and magical life surrounded by family and friends in Calgary, Alberta. When she is not writing she's walking with her furry companion Ellie, reading, cycling, sipping an Americano or tipping a pint with friends. Cathy remains ever open to new experiences and continues to travel wherever the wind takes her with unwavering faith.

# Notes

# Notes

# Notes

# Notes

CPSIA information can be obtained at www.ICGtesting.com
Printed in the USA
LVOW10s2022061016

507725LV00008B/19/P

9 780995 317901